SOUNDMACHINE

RACHEL ZUCKER

# Sound Machine

WAVE BOOKS

SEATTLE & NEW YORK

Published by Wave Books

www.wavepoetry.com

Copyright © 2019 by Rachel Zucker

Wave Books titles are distributed to the trade by

Consortium Book Sales and Distribution

Phone: 800-283-3572 / SAN 631-760X

Library of Congress Cataloging-in-Publication Data

Names: Zucker, Rachel, author.

Title: Soundmachine / Rachel Zucker.

Other titles: Sound machine

Description: First edition. | Seattle : Wave Books, [2019]

Identifiers: LCCN 2019000630

ISBN 9781940696874 (limited edition hardcover)

ISBN 9781940696867 (trade paperback)

Classification: LCC PS3626.U26 A6 2019 | DDC 811/.6—dc23

LC record available at https://lccn.loc.gov/2019000630

Designed by Crisis

Printed in the United States of America

9 8 7 6 5 4 3 2 1

First Edition

Wave Books 079

FOR **YOU**—

THANK YOU

FOR LISTENING.

*There's no cure for the shame of writing.*

—WAYNE KOESTENBAUM

*agapē állos érōs állos philia állos storgē állos*

another nother other ther o'er the her

*agapē érōs philia storgē*

SOUNDMACHINE

# SONG OF THE DARK ROOM

So it is he brings me into practice. The addressee becomes the room, the quiet—the space in which he needs me. Needs me to assuage.

So it is.

I cannot know the room of his suffering. My presence makes this a room-with-mother where sleep is possible.

The room suffers me but does not cause me suffering. Mostly.

Not quite prisoner. Not quite warden. Mother.

His fear teaches me.

Assuage is how I "put my time in."

This is as good a place as any to be. Is it?

‡

Toys & books & hours pulling words from books & putting them into the air. I resist the room's quiet embrace. It has no embrace. It is inanimate.

I resort to technologies & count down minutes.

I try to leave a residue or mother-echo that might make this a room where sleep is possible.

My desire for escape ruins everything.

I am not very good at—
is why it's called *practice*.

The nothing of the room.

‡

Of the task.

Of time.

Every night I turn off the light & take off my motherskin.

Bolt. Molt.

Not for lack of practice.

What seduction, these technologies. Junk.

In the book it's only October, but Pa is worried. The walls of the muskrat house are as thick as he's ever seen. Rain, frost & chill kill the garden, which yields only five bushels of potatoes & a few gallons of preserves. All the birds are flying south too early. Nothing—no living thing—sets down to rest in Big Slough. Strange, says Pa, Strange.

In the room it's mid-November. The boy breathes evenly after many sighs & yawns but I'm afraid to trust it. Buses idle outside. A teenager laughs wildly. The cars on Amsterdam Avenue are long waves of sound. The room could be city, country, beach, mountains but is city. Through the half-open door the radiator clanks then stops. A ticking.

The radio predicts "dimming sunshine."

3

My technology zings & beeps & brings bad news into the sky of the adult world where I am out at a poetry reading. By the time I return all is quiet. Everyone is angry with poetry.

The Husband explains all was well until the bigger boy clattered the ladder. All hell then. Glass of scotch couldn't keep the Husband calm forever, which is what he said it felt like.

Why do I resist?

This.

Do I mean poetry or motherhood?

The boy yawns & rolls over.

What is need & what is fear?

How much to give? To give in?

The boy says he's tired but feels like he cannot fall asleep. He asks me what to do.

Rest. Be comfortable in your bed, the mother says.

In a documentary about insomnia the filmmaker-narrator asks a woman who always sleeps well what it feels like. It's just a feeling, she says, There's no place I'd rather be.

"There's no place I'd rather be," I write.

The phrase "come to terms" comes to mind.

My book light flickers as the battery fails.

The boy says he's afraid if he falls asleep he'll wake up a few minutes later & find me gone. He's afraid he will have to come & find me & I'll be angry he got out of bed.

Here I am, the mother says.

Still here, she says.

One wakes the other by clattering the ladder. They are both sobbing by the time I return to check on them. The room is like a sad train car with the boys stowed in their couchettes, crying. Or are they prisoners in bunks? No, they are brothers safe in beds. When I ask them why they are crying, they say they are afraid to make me angry.

Soft carpet of the room.

I *am* angry.

The sound of my harsh growl burns my throat. I imagine slapping them.

I love you, I say, to the air, to the city, to them.

I'm not angry, the mother says.

I'm not angry, I say, starting to believe it, Try to help each other.

Their cries jangle together in weird harmony.

The boy cries. He leaves his bedroom, crosses the living room & part of the kitchen. When I hear him sniffling & shuffling I press pause on the remote & call out, We hear you . . . come on then, come in if you need to. But there's no answer, just the sound of floorboards in the hallway.

What does he want? What does he expect us to *do*? the Husband asks.

≢

I squander my time.

I listen to one crack his knuckles & shush him & use technology to see if knuckle cracking can be stopped. I listen to the boy breathe evenly for minutes & then startle awake, crying out. I shush him & feel angry & use technology to cry out to his teacher & my friends.

Minutes.

His breathing, finally, unmistakably even.

Minutes.

But I sit longer so as to regret the many errors of my ways.

≢

Outside: a swirling blizzard.

Inside: we're safe at home with our plumbing & heat high up in the city surrounded by millions.

Sleepy & safe & awake.

One reads a comic book in the top bunk, his book light glowing over the side rail. The boy sighs & stretches & makes the soft lip-smack sound he's made since birth.

The alarm at the school across the street is muffled by the tightly shut windows.

Fifteen years ago today the Husband & I went to hear live drumming at Caffe Adulis in New Haven. Later, back in my apartment, we took our clothes off. Now we are here in this honeycomb with three boys & books & comforts & consumables.

I hear the Husband in the hall. The boy breathes evenly.

The schoolroom, the lobby, the kitchen, the playroom.
The study, the waiting room, the foyer, the hallway.

The bathroom, the living room, the break room, the ante-chamber.

The dance hall, the great room, the library, the gymnasium.

The cafeteria, the sacristy, the pool hall, the operating room.

The exam room, the dorm, the cubicle, the closet.

The mudroom, the den, the boxroom, the parlor.

The larder, the sun-room, the cellar, the attic.

Alone in the late afternoon, I use my bed for something other than sleep or sex, which the experts say I should not do. I read "Sleep" by Mary Ruefle. My technology, faceup beside me, chimes & vibrates intermittently. The bed is desecrated. A makeshift library/office/snack bar where I consider the nature of the proper function of sacred space.

As a child I listened to the sounds of my parents outside my bedroom & fervently hoped to fall asleep before the house grew silent. I could not abide that silence.

Out in the world in a brightly lit gallery full of people waiting to hear Ron Padgett, my technology flashes SOS. The Husband says the boy's fast breathing alarms him & the boy's needs

9

annoy him. The boy's sadness triggers helplessness which triggers anger which results in the need for a double scotch.

I'm not crazy about the emptiness of outer space, says Padgett.

Banishèd. Banished.

Dr. Liz says, It has to be in *his* control and the way you've got it worked out, you'll never be able to stay long enough. It will never feel right to him. Say goodnight and walk away.

So, after Laura & Mary & Carrie & Grace & Ma & Pa survive a three-day blizzard in the snug, well built, in-town house, I help the boy with his relaxation exercises. We do lemon hands, cat shoulders, elephant belly, mud toes, fence belly & belly breathing.

I haven't felt like this for a long time, says the boy rolling over & yawning.

Goodnight, I say.

He catches my wrist.

Goodnight, I say, pulling away.

茾

Gasping & whimpering.

Technology cannot assuage me.

I turn to the notebook, to that stanza or room where I reside or abide, while the boy goes through it alone—gaining $x$ where $x$ stands for control & resilience or for the tangible reward he will earn if he stays in his bed.

I tiptoe through the living room to eavesdrop on his loneliness. Pen & notebook in hand I'm ready to pretend I am writing. Which I am.

The boy wants technology of his own, something with a sleek face & delicate buttons. Something that makes noise or lights up & does wonderful tricks. It's out of the question, I say. Instead, if he manages seven nights in a row, he'll get a plastic sphere that when tossed onto a laminated card pops open into the shape of a birdlike robot-transformer-being.

11

Tonight: sobbing. I write, "sobbing."

I ask a poet I know who has four children, four novels, four young adult novels, two books of poetry & a full-time job how she is able to be so productive. She responds, "Pay yourself first." She writes, "If you want the full answer call."

While the boy cries, I call.

Protect your muse time, she says.

Babies are good for poetry, she says. Prose, not so much.

No jerking off, she says.

What do you want to emerge from this mothering with? she says. What kind of body of work? When you find yourself wondering (again) if you have Cheerios, stop. Set your mind to the task.

I'll use anything to get me into the chair—jealousy, guilt, money, any slight—slights are great! she says.

When it's your writing time: no cooking, cleaning, or talking on the phone.

I'm not the one who is good at math, she says.

For a while I kept forgetting the word "ambition," she says.

The task is—

Writing.

Writing things down.

Does his need get me "into the chair"?

"Going to the chair."

What that sounds like.

When a child is sick he gets things: attention, technology, dispensations. This is called secondary gain. A mother must be very boring sometimes, not just bored.

Warden. Boring.

But how to take attention away in a way that is not punishing?

Boring warden.

The Husband & I have sex with technology. The technology makes the sex take longer but when it's over I sleep well. The next day I'm tired. In the shower I think, Can't regret that, though.

Two days later I want more sex but want my lost sleep back too. I want to finish cleaning the kitchen. I want to run to my writing like a swollen lover. Instead I go to the page & touch its erogenous zones knowing it will feel good eventually even though today it feels effortful, wifely.

"Going to the chair."

Laura is stuck at home again. The train can't get through & the town has run out of coal. There will be no school until the men clear the Tracy cut but every few days another blizzard settles.

Almanzo hides his seed wheat behind a false wall. Soon people will pay double, triple, more, for seed, for coal, for kerosene, but Almanzo doesn't want to sell. Doesn't want his brother, Royal, to sell either. Nothing is worth more to him at sowing time than seed. You can't plant money, he says.

Writing? Sex? Love? Sleep?

Family? Fear? Exhaustion?

What is the last bit of coal? Seed? Where?

Erroneous. Erogenous.

I'm writing in the kitchen away from technologies having done fifteen minutes of yoga. Supposedly inversions are as invigorating as a cup of coffee but after a short handstand I'm exhausted. Slouching & jotting away in poor alignment.

When the Husband & I prepare to go out to dinner it does not go well. The boy cries & clings to me. He says he likes the way I do lemon hands. The other cries in his room. I put him in the bath. He cries. Tell Grandma and Grandpa I want to be alone, he says & sinks under the water.

I'm not sure we should go but worry that not going will make them think their needs are great & true. We go. Their needs are great & true.

We have sex & technology again. In a way all our sex has technology if you consider the small copper wire embedded in my cervix. Meanwhile, another technology allows us to hear the baby's slightest movements four rooms away. Another technology creates a whirring white noise to drown out the cries of his brothers who cannot be bribed or threatened into silence during the baby's nap time & to drown out the trucks going by & the bus idling at our stop & the high school letting out across the street. We pump the room with noise to cover other noise. Sometimes, I imagine the baby pierced through with rays & radio waves from thousands of technologies.

Afterward: a car alarm, smooth whoosh of traffic, a mouse-like rustle in the kitchen, damn snoring.

Minute, minute, minute, minute, minute.

Let the thoughts float by, a therapist told me, years ago.

So get up & write, says my mental version of that productive poet.

Anything that gets you into the chair.

I lie here.

What the wife has tried:

Ambien, counting sheep, apple cider vinegar, warm milk, aromatherapy, oatstraw infusion, Rescue Remedy, sex, masturbation, visualization, relaxation exercises, inhale 4 hold 4 exhale 6, reading, skullcap, valerian, motherwort, chamomile, hot tea, valium, antidepressants, music, talk radio, cutting out caffeine, exercise, yoga, meditation, books on tape, rice sock, homeopathy, fear of morning, prayer.

Every minute I think: I will give him one more minute & then I will kill him. I believe he deserves to die but making him sleep in the other room seems unwifely cruel? The truth is I might have trouble sleeping even if he were not snoring but truly it is a disgusting sound.

Things the Husband has not tried:

Losing weight, using a harder pillow, seeing a doctor, strengthening his neck muscles, getting tested for sleep apnea, changing his diet, not drinking alcohol.

Still I do not wake him.

The boy wants technology, says all his friends have it. His friends have & have & they have & one even has. I say, We don't allow that in our family. I say, We do other things. I say, Every family has different rules. The boy says, You and Dad don't even look up when I talk to you, that's how I know how much you love it.

Is writing the punishment or reward? A secondary gain?

On & on goes the dark which is not really dark & the quiet which is not quiet.

I punish everyone with my insomnia.

I mean no one.

Who is myself.

Even when I am in the room I am leaving. Can he feel this? Is that why he grabs my wrist?

Even when I am not in the room I am leaving the room or thinking of leaving the room or thinking of being in the room & thinking of leaving which is a kind of leaving.

This morning I said, You treat me like a servant. I said, You leave your toys all over the place and think because I care about your feelings I'm going to take care of all your emotional and physical needs. Well you should know I feel profoundly unappreciated by everyone in this family. Then I left the room, baby on my hip.

I'm sorry, I'm so sorry, the boys said.

I almost said, Good, but said, Thank you.

The baby runs away from me whenever my attention wanders. He screams & kicks when I try to hold him.

My life feels like a waiting room.

The Husband retching.

Baby crying off & on. When I go to rock him I hear the boy in the other room moan, My stomach, my stomach . . .

I hear the other boy say, I'm sick too can't you just shut up?

I rock.

Baby's head bounces gently against my shoulder. We rock.

All the boys are asleep—for how long, who knows. The Husband rushes to the toilet. The television, on low, continues without an audience.

Snow settles on the roofs & cars but doesn't stick.

A poet sends me an envelope with instructions for a collaborative poem but I can't understand what he wants me to do.

No one describes this bitter wind as "seasonable" but why not? It's part of winter.

Tonight my body is a room filled with pathogens. I feel the lurch & sway. Please let whatever's taken hold not stick. Let there be seasons & after night, day.

## IT'S THE WORLD COMMITTING
## SUICIDE SAID ONE MOM

No, it's murder, said another.

People don't care because it's only animals dying, said Miriam.

a life spent
making marks
was what she
had been
doing she
wondered was
this also
a way of
ruining
everything

At least ART isn't gashing the precious underbelly of the planet,
said one mom.

The birds have nowhere to set down, said another.

Look how poignant that sounds, someone smirked.

    it's hard
to break
    the language

Marking. Marking time. Leslie Scalapino died.

    hard not to
*pathos pathos*
    *pathos*

Meanwhile oil was unstoppably pouring into the blue-green.

    person
or/either
    animals

*pathos pathos*

## SEVEN BEDS SIX CITIES EIGHT WEEKS

Yesterday I began writing a poem in *The Book of Nothing* called "Facebook or the End of Espionage." The first line, "They already know all about you," is all I wrote. Then, nothing.

By "yesterday" I might mean last year. This is a characteristic problem with reportage.

Many true things are difficult to write or offensive to others but *The Book of Nothing* is not intended for a general audience so I can write anything but I suspect the idea of a "general audience" might be offensive & fallacious.

For example, I got into trouble with a collaborative, collaged, lyric essay that I wrote with AG. We hurt B's feelings so we apologized & took out all references to B. (B's not even her real initial.) Even so, B said she was shocked & saddened that we'd used her story as "creative fodder."

I take *The Book of Nothing* with me when I leave the city. It isn't heavy, is hardly anything. Even so, everything is changed by its presence.

Once I told someone, Poetry is my way of making sense of my surroundings, of paying attention.

I might have said that more than once or never. I can't remember. And to whom?

Fodder:
1) something fed to domestic animals; especially: coarse food for cattle, horses, or sheep
2) inferior or readily available material used to supply a heavy demand

Whereas writing prose, I said, requires that I shut out the world. I could be anywhere.

Supposedly, Jonathan Franzen wrote *The Corrections* blindfolded in his basement. Or was that David Foster Wallace writing *Girl with Curious Hair*?

Jim Galvin said, Writing prose is just typing. He said it right after I'd told him how much I liked his book *The Meadow*.

*The Book of Nothing* briefly adopts a pastoral soundtrack but cannot maintain it.

*The Book of Nothing* is not a poem. It is also not not a poem. It is nothing, after all.

My friend Ilana has fluid in the tissue around her lungs & heart that cannot be drained. Also a tumor in her brain & several metastases. But she is living. Not nothing. Not for nothing. Nothing to sneeze at. Nothing is as nothing does.

I knew something was wrong but didn't want to ask anyone for fear of seeming like the stupid city girl. The cow's belly was twitching & convulsing & her eyes were closed, her neck at an odd angle. The other three cows in the pen gathered around her as I approached & then scattered to the far edges when I came closer. Finally I worked up the courage to ask the young woman sweeping out another pen & she told me the cow had been treated earlier in the day & just as she said that the cow keeled over & fell, with a thud, on her side.

Thud, I thought, "Thud" is the name of that sound.

The cow had been treated for pneumonia & was lying on her side in the mucky pen. One thousand pounds down, I thought. Her breath was white vapor around her snout. Labored breathing, someone said. The cow grew quiet, then shuddered & relaxed.

Might not make it, said the camp director who'd been called over by a counselor.

That cow's dead, I thought.

Might not make it till evening, he said.

The poet John Ashbery is nowhere in sight but as far as I know, living.

My friend has decided to decide by the end of June whether to get married or break up. What if the fact that I have so many doubts means getting married is the wrong choice? he asks. I try to explain the idea of a characteristic dilemma. I say, How could you *not* have doubts?

I've been married for eleven years & thirteen days.

I am asked to write a blurb for a book by a poet I know slightly. I like the lines, "this room / will always be the ghost of right now for as long as we carry it." I like the whole book, which has a spooky, sensual immediacy. But I hate writing blurbs.

CNN online reports that a seven-year-old boy went swimming with his family at a local pond. On the way home the boy seemed unusually tired & asked to lie down. A few hours later the boy died, in his bed, from drowning. The story says unusual fatigue or changes in behavior can be signs of water in the lungs.

I decide this story has no place in *The Book of Nothing* but it's too late now.

I decide to write a series of prose poems about everything I can remember from my childhood. Each poem will be a distilled snapshot of my past which disappears as I watch. I cannot think of a single memory.

I write: Does one's memory degrade more quickly and more completely if one has children?

The director climbed into the pen & patted the cow's belly & then kicked the cow. Not gently, not hard, in the side. He covered the animal with a blue tarp just as the Peapods & Seedlings entered the barn to pick up their backpacks.

Yesterday I saw a cow die, I say to my friend Erin on the phone. I'm sure that will end up in a poem, Erin says.

I decide that this exchange is how I will begin the essay about teaching poetry workshops that I've been asked to write, if I decide to write that essay. I might decline the assignment in which case I should stop wasting time thinking about how to support my argument that description is fundamental to good writing.

There are at least ten frogs in a small pond near the house we're renting in Brunswick, Maine. When I venture near the pond the frogs stop moving & stop making sounds so it is difficult to count them. For seventeen days I've been trying to describe the sound they make. It is nothing like "ribbit" or "croak" or any of the other onomatopoeias we use for frog noises.

Finally, it comes to me: they sound like a wide rubber band snapping once—a quick, low, single twang—a boing, reverb without consonants.

*The Book of Nothing* is like a postcard sent to no one, with a frog's real sound.

*The Book of Nothing* sounds Buddhist but is not. At least it is not intended to be Buddhist as such although Buddhism or some watered-down version of Buddhist principles has seeped into art's groundwater, so maybe it's unavoidable.

They say memory is the spring that feeds good literature. Being memory impaired I can't say who "they" is or if, indeed, anyone actually said this. Let's hope it's not true.

I give my son a notebook for his ninth birthday.
What do you think . . . what kinds of things should I . . .? he asks.
Nothing, I say, Unless you want to.
What's in it? says my other son, pointing at the notebook.
Nothing, the birthday boy says, looking down.

I think about the difference between lemonade & *citron pressé*. I think about the fact that I like scrambled eggs but not omelets, prefer peaches to nectarines but only if they're cut into slices. I think about the phrase "constituent elements."

Paris exists but I do not go there.

"Yesterday I saw a cow die," I write, beginning a microessay on teaching poetry. In truth, I began the essay fourteen days after watching the cow die; since then, no further progress. Further progress on the essay, I mean. I'm not talking about the cow's progress.

Yesterday I was informed that the conference panel proposal that includes me as a participant has been accepted. The panel is about representing the self in writing. Here's what I have to say about that: [                                    ]

Memory is a funny word. It applies both to the power of remembering & to what is remembered. The word comes from the Latin *memoria* (a historical account), from *memor* (mindful) & from the Old English *mimor* (well-known) & from the Greek *merm ra* (care).

For this reason I often avoid greeting someone I know but whose name I might not recall.

In Denver the air is thin & fragile. Even in the shade of trees I feel exposed to the sun's relentlessness. I am living, for eleven days, in my mother-in-law's home.

Was there something you were planning to do today? my mother-in-law asks after explaining she cannot watch the baby.

*The Book of Nothing* will not address the purpose of life.

*The Book of Nothing* would address the question "what is work," if there were time for such investigations.

I have nothing nice to say about Denver.

The poet likes the blurb I wrote. The microessay is still one sentence, but I changed "yesterday" to "today" for a greater sense of immediacy.

What is work?

As instructed, I have registered my treatment for a reality-TV game show with the Screen Writers Guild. It has been six weeks since the prospective agent promised to call me the next day. I am also waiting for a response from a parenting magazine about an essay I wrote about teaching poetry to young children. Tomorrow we leave for Wisconsin.

On Ilana's caringbridge.org site she describes her treatment & symptoms & state of mind. In *The Book of Nothing* I write: "REALITY SHOW."

Specifically I am trying to decide whether or not to return to the novel I began writing four years ago & dropped after sixty pages & two years or whether to work on my nonfiction memoir that three agents praised & rejected. Or to start something new. Or not to write at all. Hence or instead, *The Book of Nothing*.

Wayne says this is a characteristic problem.

Arielle says I'm a whiner. She likes to hear my new poems over the phone but finds my angst over what to do next exhausting.

I have no new poems, which exhausts me.

What is work?

Poetry is a way of connecting to the world, of noticing, of placing myself, I said to someone while teaching or in an interview or else I read it somewhere in which case: plagiarism.

My memory. This memory.

Perhaps eventually I will forget my own characteristic dilemmas at which point memory loss will be the only characteristic dilemma left.

I read somewhere that fetal cells remain in the mother for twenty-seven years after birth. Or seventeen. I can't remember what conclusion or analogy I was about to draw from this fact.

It's true that my body has a quality of excess, unnecessariness, but is, at the same time, useful, productive.

Feeling is *part* of the form, of proper form. Is that an argument? Or a desire?

You can't eat a diseased animal so in this sense the cow is wasted. If the purpose of the animal is to provide sustenance for other animals, which is not its purpose.

Fodder.

I have nothing to say about "the speaker." Instead I go swimming in the pool on my husband's grandmother's property in Lakewood, Colorado, in my ill-fitting swimsuit. Unshaven, untoned, slightly panicky in the goggled blue, the muffled solitude of submergence. City girl with poor form & pale skin—spectacle for none to witness.

What I like is the long, underwater glide as I push off from the wall.

What I like are the amoeba-shaped blue tiles along the bottom & sides of the rectangular pool. The chipped tiles, the places where a tile is missing.

In the car my son reads to himself. Every once in a while, he spells out a word he doesn't recognize. I like how the possibilities of the first few letters narrow with each subsequent letter until the word takes shape & becomes meaningful.

I go to a yoga class but the chanting & call-&-response prayer agitate me. After chanting we sit in silence, breathing & then the teacher reads a long passage from a book about the difference between experience & experiencing. Experience is between life & experiencing. Experience is time-bound, on a continuum. The mind is a product of experience. Thought is a product of the mind. The idea is to rid oneself of thought, of memory, of mind, of all time-bound experience so as to approach experiencing the here & now. It is hard to follow all this because I am thinking of *The Book of Nothing* & how I will describe all this nonsense in *The Book of Nothing*, which is a way of thinking about the future (now present) & therefore a failed moment of experiencing.

Brunswick, Denver, Sturgeon Bay, Greenport.

Last night I dreamed my husband was carrying a blond child about three years old. The child was crying. I took the child in my arms but could not comfort her. Around five a.m. I heard someone say Mother, clearly & out loud. The sound woke me. I looked at the clock & at my sleeping husband thinking I'd never heard him talk in his sleep & how funny it was that he'd said Mother. Just as I was dozing off, I heard the word "Mother" again. It was not my husband's voice. I heard whispering. I sat up in bed & put my ear to the wall that separated our bedroom from the room our boys were sleeping in—all quiet. Neither of them has ever called me "Mother."

I keep a dream notebook & often write down my dreams. By often I mean rarely. By rarely I mean lately.

Only now, writing this down, do I make a connection between the child in the dream & my friend Ilana, who is dying.

My mother forgets things. Small things like where she put her glasses or camera & bigger things like my husband's last name. But she denies this. I did *not* say Gordon—you misheard me, she says. Or, You never told me that! When clearly I did. On the other hand, she memorizes long stories that she tells to rapt audiences.

I meant: forgot, denied, said, memorized. I meant, May her blessing be a memory. I mean, May her memory be a blessing.

How memory is equated with caring. "Thanks for asking."

I take the baby to our apartment to pick up our mail. The baby seems to have no recollection of our apartment & makes no effort to see his room while I sit by the front door sorting junk mail. Some people call this The Wonder Years.

What the baby remembers is me. And his father. And his brothers. This is an important survival skill but annoying when I want to leave him in the care of others.

When I write "the baby" it is like writing "yesterday" or, one day, "years ago."

I still think of the pool in Lakewood as Emmett's pool. He kept it hot & after his heart-valve replacement surgery, walked back & forth along the short side of the shallow end for hydrotherapy. I think about sitting with his coffin in the basement of the funeral home & how I spent my allotted hour agonizing over whether to open the coffin to see his body one last time.

Whether I opened the casket or not is recorded in *The Book of Nothing*. For prosperity. I think I mean posterity.

In an email Ilana tells me that her childhood dog has come to be with her & has been by her side all morning. This is not a dream. Neither the dog nor the email.

Good to remember: one can die from poisoned berries. See the movie *Into the Wild* based on the book by Jon Krakauer based on the story of Christopher McCandless whose name I had to look up when I typed this three months later. The original text of *The Book of Nothing* says, "based on the life of _____."

More & more I am drawn to the literal. Is this a fad? A developmental stage? A characteristic dilemma?

On my favorite radio show there is a piece about a woman in her thirties who asked, at a party: Are unicorns still endangered or have they finally become extinct? The silence that followed was what clued her in.

Or perhaps I mean the surreal. It's hard to tell.

By radio show I mean podcast.

Seven beds in six cities in eight weeks including the Newark airport hotel when we missed our connecting flight.

Now here.

A lack of childcare changes *The Book of Nothing*. Lessens it. Increases its appeal. The baby puts things in his mouth & cannot be trusted.

By "baby" I mean "when." When there was/he was a baby.

It is five a.m. It is still 5 A.M.

Last night on the way home—[the baby swallows stories, words, all my language with his promiscuous mouth]

     —what was I saying?

This morning Ilana died.

Ilana died, this morning.

I write: "Ilana died." I cross it out. I write it again.

Perhaps *The Book of Nothing* is a notebook not a book. One small note changing everything.

On the ferry home my son says, I hate you. He'd battled his brother over the crinkly paper around his cookie & lost. When he pulled away from me, I yanked him close. Not safe, I said.

Evening. Half moon, hidden stars. The ocean again.

What will I wear to the funeral? I ask *The Book of Nothing*. Nothing, it says. Or, it says nothing.

During the service, *The Book of Nothing* sits quietly in the passenger seat of the rented Kia. Later, during the shiva, lies in the trunk with the clothes & diapers.

Three houses down from the one we're renting two houses catch fire. We watch. There is no one, thank god, inside. A neighbor hoses down everything between her house & the ones on fire. We watch as the first house burns. We watch as the house next to it goes up in flames. We watch as the volunteer squads arrive from Greenport, Southold, Cutchogue, Orient, Riverhead. We watch as a special ladder truck arrives & lowers a firefighter

onto the roof. We watch as the firefighter sits astride the gable
& tries to cut through the roof with a handheld chainsaw. The
buildings burn.

*The Book of Nothing* is

The very bad smell as the vinyl siding collapses away from the
wooden bones.

nothing if not _____.

When it is all over a firefighter puts a helmet on the baby, who
is wearing only a diaper, not even shoes & who is not afraid of
the fire or of anything because he knows so little, almost noth-
ing & we take a photo.

The stars last night, after a clear day.

A week ago Ilana died.

Now I mean a month.

Later I will mean years. I cannot make sense of this.

The baby has words: "wawa" (water), "haa" (hat), "zeze" (zebra), "heh" (head), "baw" (ball), "moe" (more), "nuh" (nurse), "tees" (trees), as well as names: Mawma, Dada, Bruba, Bapah & many animal sounds.

"Baby" once meant today or yesterday. Now means years ago.

On one side of us is a house, then two burned houses. On the other side, just across the street, a graveyard. The house is musty & filled with knickknacks & junktoys, screens off their tracks, doors swelled past closing. Here, I sleep well. The nights are cool. The stars.

Called out of yoga, I'm at the hospital waiting for A to have her cesarean. It's too quiet. Will I be able to hear the baby cry through the closed door of the OR? I am A's doula. I am supporting her by standing outside the closed door. This is what I am permitted.

Ilana is still dead.

The city.

October is almost over & I have not written a novel or part of a novel or a series of poems about memory. I have not written a microessay about teaching. I have not written a microessay about the line but have promised to do so. I wrote one new poem about waking up early with the baby but it's a silly little song-poem & its sweetness bothers me. I have not written an essay about Alice Notley or the email to the agent outlining the "what happened" version of my nonfiction book, which according to her is weak on plot. I spent a few weeks making a nine-minute movie about the baby's home birth & posted it to youtube. It's gotten 49,580 hits in the past four weeks, which makes it my most successful publication.

New York is gray & bleak.

This morning I woke up & thought, Ilana, are you *still* dead?

I write: "Today David Foster Wallace hung himself." That's what day this was. Later I will change this to "hanged" but doing so won't change anything for David Foster Wallace.

Once I attended a tribute reading for Elizabeth Bishop. Jorie Graham helped John Ashbery onto the stage & John Ashbery cried when he read Bishop's poem. Did I dream that? No. But I can't remember when or where it was & which poem of Bishop's Ashbery read. It was at least ten years ago. Ashbery seemed old then. I remember thinking, as I looked at him, He's next. But he wasn't.

I gave my books of poetry to Ilana as gifts but doubt she read them. This has to do with the problem of a general audience.

The summer disappears into photographs. Houses & hours on airplanes.

The City blocks out almost everything I am.

Meanwhile: Obama, the economy, famous & less famous suicides, the Library of America publishes Ashbery's collected poems on the day the baby I miscarried would have been two years old & my living baby turns sixteen months & two days. So what?

Like a fish I grow to fit my environment in this case apartment in which I sit at my computer & listen to the MP3 of Cat Stevens singing "if you want to be me, be me" from Ilana's favorite song while I do not write anything for my panel about the relationship between self & poet & do not work on my novel or poems about memory or from memory. I do not write about Ilana who was my doula teacher or John Ashbery who is a poet, one of whom is dead & one of whom is alive, or about David Foster Wallace who is dead or about Alice Notley who is alive & who was not my teacher but who said, There has to be a way to talk about oneself without narcissism & said, That's only one story: what you remember.

## HOURS DAYS YEARS
## UNMOOR THEIR ORBITS

Tonight I'm cleaning baby portobellos just for you, my young activist.

I'm wiping the dirty tops with a damp cloth as carefully as I used to rinse raspberries for you to adorn your fingertips before eating each blood-red prize.

These days you rarely look me in the eye & your long, shagged hair hides your smile.

I don't expect you to remember or understand the many ways I've kept you alive or the life my love for you has made me live.

**I CAN BARELY STAND TO GO TO
WEDDINGS & DARE NOT DRINK
LEST I SAY TO BRIDE OR GROOM
"HOW TERRIBLE TO LOVE SO MUCH
THAT ONLY THE FANTASY OF THE
ANNIHILATION OF HUMANITY IS A
COMFORT BECAUSE PREFERABLE TO
THE LOSS OF THE ONE BELOVÈD"**

Today I took a group of students to the Louvre to see Venus de Milo & her pert, exquisite breasts. I read them Emma Lazarus's poem to grief-struck Heinrich Heine & we talked about ekphrastic this & that. But it was a marriage of convenience for me, Emma, Heinrich & Venus.

Later I dragged my sons to L'Orangerie to see Monet at Giverny painting his way through WWI. I imagined my father's father circa 1934 feather in hat & my father's mother, small & prim—can almost hear them whispering in Yiddish—my grandmother understanding the paintings, my grandfather trying to.

Up close they make no sense, my son said, pointing to the paintings.

My grandparents died half my lifetime ago & the missing—

knife? corset? sting?

What metaphor suffices?

Would that I were lapis lazuli & could be ground & pressed into trees, water, lily pads, sky but *désolée* am not.

Now, at le Jardin, a child sobs his way around the carousel & another cries because he is too young to ride. My youngest son shouts nonsense in a French accent at children who pay him no attention. The mothers in their *jolis* hats laugh & touch one another on the elbows while the operator in the smoke-filled booth cares only that the tickets are in order. I watch the ride go on & on knowing it will stop.

# ROUGH WATERS

The lesson to learn is _____, Jer says.
Or, maybe the lesson to learn is _____.


Down at the beach a woman is pulling a young boy on a body-
board. The boy is fair with blond hair. The woman looks Hawai-
ian. She is thin & wears a bikini. She pulls the boy fast, with
abandon. The boy slips off the board into the sand, pulls himself
up, toddles back to the board, sits down. The woman pulls the
board. The boy laughs. The woman laughs. He flips off, onto the
sand. She kneels to help him, laughing.


Everyone is worried about someone else.
Everyone is worried that the person worrying about someone
else should be more worried about himself.


Worried is not the right word.


In the grassy area in front of the hotel, a photographer is taking
photographs of a bride & groom or two people dressed as bride

& groom. They are playing a staged game of peekaboo around two trees growing out of one hole in the ground. Or perhaps it is one tree with a split trunk.

**Some people are getting married today** I text D.
**Maybe don't tell them what they have in store** D texts back.
**Hah** I text.

In the shallows a man is teaching a toddler to stand on a surfboard. The boy wears a safety vest. The boy falls, face first, into the water. The man scoops him up by the elbow & puts him back on the board. The boy kneels on the board, blinking.

Why don't I feel—? I ask K.
Don't worry about it, she says, Lots of reasons.

Everyone asks me if I'm Hawaiian, says the woman who looks Hawaiian to a woman swimming next to her. I drift closer. I want to hear what she is saying. Is she saying that she is not Hawaiian? Or that she is? I want to know how she feels about the fact that everyone asks her if she is Hawaiian. I want to ask her if she is Hawaiian.

B wants to know: Did they find out what happened?
What happened is he died.

But did they find out?

What?

How?

What?

What happened?

He died.


Perhaps the lesson is to love with abandon, Jer says.

No, that's not right. He didn't say "abandon."

What did he say? "Wildly"?

Love. Love in some way.

Some way other than the way one mostly loves or has loved.


Or, says Jer, It's possible life is a waste of time and full of suf-
fering.


Why do I feel ___? Less—? Not—? Is it shock?


Everyone is looking at everyone else.

Everyone is holding up.

Everyone is devastated.

Everyone is saying it is worse for _____.

It *is* worse for _____.

There's no denying.

Well, says C, at lunch, What if there *was* a contest for most terrible?

Count me in, jokes B.

Count me out, jokes C.


The word "surreal." Also: "impossible," "terrible," "unimaginable."


But isn't he the last person one could imagine dying? B asks C.

C looks uncomfortable, a little offended.

Because of his physical presence, says B.

Yes, yes, of course, says C.


"I'm not good in person," I write to T. "Perhaps this is why I am a writer. Perhaps this is why I don't have many friends. Perhaps this is why I so admired and idealized him—he had so many friends, was so good in person."


Don't read this, I say, when I give T the letter. I mean, *do* read it if you want to but *when* you want to, maybe *after* or later or when I leave or not at all if you don't want to . . . I'm not . . . it's just . . . *impossible*, I say.

When I talk it's like sliding down a rope. I descend ungracefully, my legs unable to grip, arms too weak to bear my own weight, hands burning, the word "impossible" a blunt mat onto which I fall.

The surfers are way out in the bigger waves. The swimmers, closer in. In the middle distance a few kayaks & people on paddleboards. The ocean has different areas with different qualities. It is not one thing. Wave patterns change here & there. There are flags & markers & signs.

I am alive to see this.
I am here to see this because he is not alive.

At lunch G describes swimming the English Channel.
Fifteen forty-five, he says.
He swam for fifteen hours and forty-five minutes.
Impossible, I think.

The sign on the beach says Strong Current. I stay close to the shore. I feel nothing. The water is buoyant & calm. No current. There are young children farther out than I am. I float on my back in the knee-deep water where I feel nothing.

Some swimmers swim out to the far, far flag.
How will they get back, I wonder.
I watch them swim with smooth, long strokes.

This is not even the most beautiful beach, a man on the beach says.
I know, I never come here, a woman replies.

My device tells me I am 4,957 miles away from the people for whom, if I died, it would be worst for them. No question. Everyone would agree.

I think there's no lesson to be learned from his death about how *not* to die, I say.
No, says K, Impossible.

Did they find out what happened? people keep asking.

Everyone says everyone else is in shock.
This is how it occurs to me I might be in shock.
It doesn't feel like shock, I say to K. It feels like ____.

G says it would never have occurred to him that anything like this could happen. He was such a strong swimmer and had trained and done stuff like this before, G says.

But now everyone is thinking that something like this *could* happen to them or to anyone because it has just happened.

Maybe, I say to J, I just need to believe when I look into my kids' eyes that they would be OK. I need to believe that. So somehow *this* has to be OK?
What? says J. This is *not* OK.
People die, I say.
You've been through a lot, J says.

I lie in bed thinking about how the word *everyone* is singular. How little sense this makes.

And beyond the surfers: sailboats.

It is hot & bright & hot & bright even though the people whose deaths would be worst for me are in their night with many cooling machines clanking & chugging. Their sun is with me now. Our one sun.

Is it because I have no grief left? I ask L & K & J.
Or because I am middle-aged?
Or because we didn't see each other often?
Or because I can't bear to ____?
Or because he had a good life?

In the ocean a man holds a girl too old to be held the way he is holding her. It doesn't make sense until I realize she can't move her arms & legs on her own. Then it makes sense: the way he is holding her against his leg, under her arms, her arms limp & long, not moving.

He lets the girl slip & she swims away effortlessly. The girl swims to the man & climbs on his back. The man swims, his face underwater with the girl on his back. She waves her arms. I watch. She makes her own sense.

Take me across the water, various animals ask Turtle in many stories.
What story is this?
What animal am I?

I lose track of whether the same swimmers who swim out swim back.

Why do I need to sit here & figure out how I feel?
How I feel is: this may be the first time in my life I don't know how I feel.
Is that a feeling?

And who is watching to see if all the swimmers that go out come back?
The surfers? The boats?

Sometimes, says C, I want to go up to those guys who ride motorcycles without helmets & say to them, Hey, someone loves you!

People die, I think. People die.

Mostly I do not say this aloud.
Sometimes I do.

You're wrong, says he for whom my death would be worst. He was in the middle of some very big projects. Raising his kids, for one. And if you don't finish that . . .

Please let me know, everyone says.
If there is anything I can do, everyone says.
There is nothing to do, we all say back & forth to one another.

Thank you for coming.

I'm so glad I could be here.

Under these circumstances.

∿

In the home movies he looks like himself. And is so funny.

I forget the definition of surreal. Is it less than real or more than real? Underreal? No, that would be subreal. I am so tired.

His voice is the same.
The same as what?

Funny. Loved.

Someone makes wonderful dal.

Everyone wants everyone else to eat. Everyone wants everyone else to sit down & not clean up. There are skirmishes in the kitchen for the sponge, for the pyrex, for the chance to take out the trash.

Everyone thinks it might be time to clear out & go home.

I am waiting for it to hit me.

∿

C asks L how anyone can help T but L says the main thing is the children and it is worse for them.

Later I ask C if he is OK. He says he is OK but it is worse for L.

Everyone wonders when everyone else will really fall apart. Everyone is relieved at how everyone else is holding up but no one believes this can or even should last, this holding up, which is not to say that anyone wants anyone else not to hold up unless holding up is a kind of falseness that will result in some kind of worse future falling apart in which case perhaps everyone else should go ahead & fall apart before everyone else goes home because everyone is very worried about what will happen when everyone goes home.

Do you think this will change their relationship to the ocean? I ask.

All the swimming & surfing friends say that what happened to him had nothing to do with the ocean.

Everyone wants to know whether to wash the plastic forks. No, is the answer. Throw them out.

It *is* the ocean, someone says every once in a while.

B keeps his feelings about religion private at a time like this.

No one says: I can feel his presence.
Everyone says: I keep expecting to see him. Everyone says: I see him everywhere. While watching the home videos from 1989 someone says, He wears those same shorts to this day.

His body was cremated today. This day.
Today.

The ones for whom my death would be worst are getting back the sun. It is almost up for them & dark for me. They will do their important things that people do, like soccer & eating. They will make messes but no one will beg them oh please let me clean that up or say please, please sit down. No one will worry if they are getting any sleep at all.

Thank you for your letter, T says.
I fumble with word-sounds as if my mouth is filled with change.
Let's leave it at that, T says & I touch her shoulder in a creepy way.
We hug & the hug makes sense: the shape of it.

∿

Down at the beach women are doing yoga on surfboards, bob-
bing in the shallows. The rock formations below the water are
visible today. The water is light green, the rocks grayish blue.

A man with a snorkel waves a metal detector underwater &
flattens his masked face to the surface.

The women on the boards make shapes singly or in pairs. One
stands on her head & opens her legs in a perfect V. The board
rocks. Her body holds.

∿

Everyone is trying to stay out of everyone's way. Everyone
wants to support everyone else. Everyone wishes that everyone
else would be clearer about what they want.

All the stories are eulogies now.

The big waves break beyond the flag. By the time the water
reaches the middle distance there is almost no surf at all, just
a small tumble where the water edges the beach.

The sand darkens & lightens as the water creeps up & draws away, furls & unfurls.

I sit on the balcony & read *Tape for the Turn of the Year* by A. R. Ammons, where it is winter & 1963 & bitter cold in Ithaca in the house of this poet who doesn't like to travel.

> you—who are you? How do
> I feel about you?
> do I hate it that I love
> to be tied to you by love?
>             untied, wd I be free
>        or lost?

Everyone wonders how everyone else is really feeling. Everyone is worried about saying the wrong thing. Each new person arrives with a strange, furrowed look, their brows pinched in the unspoken question of how to be & of what it will be like to be with everyone in this paradise.

Affable. Comfortable. Fearless. Funny. All the adjectives are elegiac.

I'm not saying I wish everyone were crying.

I'm not saying anything, really.

For once I'm not talking too much.


The sound of the ocean through the closed glass hotel-room doors.


Inside, emptiness.


B is always waiting for me. Everyone is always thinking they should spend more time with one another but also wanting to be alone & wanting everyone else to leave them alone & not knowing how to say that. Or maybe that's only what I want.

∿


Farther down the beach the ocean slams against a stone wall. A blond woman in a bikini sits cross-legged on the wall, her middle fingers touching thumbs, palms resting on her knees. A man crouches, camera ready, waiting for the water to hit the wall & spray up behind her like a huge aquatic fan. She smiles apolo getically. I wait for the water to hit & rise up so the man can snap the photo.


The main thing, B says, Is being here.

On a narrow stone pier a crowd of people throw old leis into the ocean.
The lifeguard walks out to speak to them.

Are you happy you came? B asks.

The main thing is being here, B says.

Everyone here is in the present tense.
Everyone slips into the past when he was alive & everyone could speak of him in present tense.

In this way we are always in the wrong time zone.
In the past when he was present & in the present where he is not.

∿

It's so hot but you don't want to swim?
No, says B, It feels—. B shrugs. I'm not even sitting shiva, B says.

Five thousand miles away my for-whom-my-death-would-be-worst is putting my youngest son to sleep. Also the nieces are sleeping over.

Down at the beach two men bob in the water.
I hope we're not getting fucking burned to death, one says to
the other.
Dude, the other one says.

I float on my back & think about the word *muffle*. I stay near
the shore.

Was it a nice swim? a stranger asks as I walk toward my towel.
Impossible, I say.
Excuse me? the man says.
It is impossibly nice, I say.
The man smiles & nods.

∿

What story is this?
What animal am I?

∿

In the morning the ocean is blue until the sun rises above the
roof of the hotel. Then it is green.

Everyone gets ready to head out into the theater of mourning
by putting on outfits & folding their eulogies & putting packets
of tissues in their purses & pockets.

The kids. The kids. T.

A long sharp window of light—the opposite of a shadow—strikes the water from between two hotels. Which color is more real, the moody blue or placid green?

Everyone is dressed & ready & aching all over. Everything hurts us.

The pain is a long, thin window of light.

Everyone goes now into the auditorium where everyone has a different god or no god & there is no body & a slideshow.

In which there is crying. In which there is laughter. In which there is music. In which no one asks how this could have happened. In which no one cries out woe is me. In which everyone says he was magnificent & massive & loving & kind.

There is no safety patrol to pull anyone out of these waters or photos or words or music & his banjo up on the stage & his colleagues & friends & daughter at the podium his son & other daughter watching & his brothers & his mother & his father & his wife.

His life now the story of it & ours going on without him into this, into this state of being & absence & abandon in which abandon is how one should love not how one is left or leaves. We are in these waters now & we swim out calling his name.

# DEATH PROJECT [POEM]

*This will help.*

Smaller & smaller. Skin looser.
The healthy are afraid to mention, afraid to say what is happening.
As soon as you think you know what is happening, you do not know.
What is happening?
It is happening to you, afraid it is happening to you.

*This will help you.*

There is nothing surprising except everything you are feeling.
The giving way.
The way everything is predictable but never to you, exactly.

*This will help you to arrange, hold, stem, reconstruct words into meaningful predictive protective—*

The made.

The made way for.

The giving way to.

Words makes you watch.

What? your son says into the dark from bed, You're saying I will cease to exist? Isn't there any way to stop this?

> be there watch stay wait into the dark or the dim light into the whatever light there is // as the breathing changes (yours the mothers the fathers the grand-mothers the other grandmothers the other mother the machine) / stay here / you want to go out scream-ing into the diminished environment / the way "we" have ruined everything & the we that wants desper-ately against everything you know is true to be any-thing other than I //

> you need to // stay // *stay* // *here* // see what is hap-pening to the diminishing giving way / giving away / words reach / you need words to reach into / where there are no words / "there are no words" /

> people always say *those* words / those words are the words people say /

stay there // *stay* // in the unmade made room in the
still cardiac place / inside the loosening skin / the polar
icecaps giving way / the giving way the world warm-
ing // the bodies one by one losing heat inside the giv-
ing way / for a brief time / he she they / we / treated
each other as theirselves / the polar diminishing ani-
mals the vanishing / we were once hearty with a sense
of smell touch vision feeling taste future /

That's it, right? The belief that there will be something that does
not warm or cool, a second more of—

After the success & controversy surrounding her *Immediate
Family* photographs Sally Mann decided it was time to stop tak-
ing pictures of her three children & move on to something else.

But what? She looked. She waited.

One day, as she stood in the kitchen of her Virginia farmhouse
the sheriff called & told her there was an escaped convict on
her farm & she had to get out. At that very moment she saw
him. Running. Running toward the house. Police running after
him as he ran toward the house. He shot. They shot. Police shot-
gun hit to the hip. The convict turned his pistol on himself.

Later she touched the pool of blood near the convict's head. It was surprisingly dark, she said. When she touched it, it moved, she said. She saw the ground take a sip.

She began to photograph the place where he died. She began to go to the places nearby where many had died long or short ago & photograph those places using the materials photographers had used during the Civil War.

Then what?

*What Remains.*

She was given access to a facility in which someone was studying the decomposition of human bodies. A facility in which human bodies were strewn, laid out, in the open. Fly eaten, maggoted, at various stages. Sally Mann made photographs of these bodies, plate after plate.

Then closeup exposures of the children again but not children anymore rather living subjects & similar—like her face but not her face—living, ethereal from the old-timey process. The lens open, open, hold, hold, stay, stay, stay, OK.

Prints made & framed, years of work created & ready when the Pace Gallery in NY canceled the show at the last minute. Who wants to hang photos of dead bodies on their walls? Who would buy these? It is the only time in the film that Sally Mann cries on camera. Not when speaking about the death of her father or her favorite dog or the threats to charge her with child pornography & take her children & her equipment into custody.

I think it [the work] is important, but maybe it isn't, Sally Mann says. Maybe it's important but no one wants to see it? she says, wiping her nose.


The inclusion of this information helps you navigate the aboutness of this poem, maybe the whyness. It is a transmission from the poet, a kind of de/composition. The poet is not the you, is no I either.

[ here ] [now] the poet takes this opportunity to say:

This morning standing in the hot shower, hoping heat would enter my body & be trapped there even for an hour, even minutes, knowing it would dissipate, unlike the arsenic mercury BPAs my cells won't give up—

*which is the poem?*

*which is the poet?*

*how does anything get inside anything else?*
*anyone? how do you get it out?*


You're telling me I will cease to exist? the boy asks.

> *into the night into you the night pressing you*
> *in the dark his breathing catching uneven*

Not for a very long time, you say.

> but it is a short time // it is no // time // there are rocks
> & trees & polar icecaps // it is no time at all / it is too
> short

It will feel like a long, long time, you tell the boy.

Maybe you will be ready, you tell the boy.

maybe you will feel ready to give way to let your / mus-
cles give way even your heart to stop / beating let go
of / the sense of future // the holding tight to clutch-
ing to others the we / clinging / the way the poet clings
to the boy the night the voice the words

*This will help you die—*

asserts the poet not sure of anything—

*—take it take it take this take it* she says

the mark you make in the present // weight of your
body // way you press into the present your in out of
oxygen carbon nitrogen / the gravity that holds you
to this planet / is a clinging to others / even as you
repel / the fabric of / the only perceivables are //      //
this is the meaning of

the music of the room / live musicians / the nurse
reading a book into / the room the stranger the doctor
the daughter the friend / the gurney down the
brightly lit / the home bedroom with hospital bed /

the box the plot the visiting hour // the hours // the breath //

what did you think was going to happen? / did you think there was another way of bearing up? / a giving way the giving way to / the suddenly the slowly / the you saying someone else's pain is worse / is lesser / is a blessing / the you who dreams the gone-away souls back again /

the you who goes on toward your own room bed stranger doctor daughter friend

We has made paintings of this. Paintings of all the stories in the world. And none of all the stories in the world are the stories of what happens next, only the stories of "we in the face of."

She wrote *fact of*, but that is the face of it, the fact of it is not faceable. You never can know what it was like for anyone else You never know birth fear pleasure of anyone else. You have always been alone in the dark with a young boy asking you:

You have always been alone in a room wanting any small other to ask anything of you which is the only thing that makes you sure you're you.

[there]
[here]

hearing a you, the you you are

Hasn't anyone ever tried to stop this? the boy asks.

Yes, you say, People try but—

What happens after? he asks.

No one knows, you say.

After all this time? he asks. Really?

Really, you say.

And you're doing nothing about this?

You make a poem called "This Poem Will Help You Die" to hang on the wall for no one to buy. *Here*, says the poem, *Take it, take it in*.

## LET THE WORLD UNFURL
## ONE WORD AT A TIME

A mother holds the sky at bay. Baby on her back. Another on the way.
The key to this is the seat of the throne of the thumb of the rule of power.

Take my bones, she says, And with your bright light make me a lady-homunculus.

Go away geniuses & strong-armed bullies. Put down your rusted jousts.
By lace & smoke & note & thrum we cry out to one another.

# SNAPSHOT

The Husband & I stand next to each other: not speaking, sometimes speaking.

*See?* Asks the photograph. A closeness or almostness?

The photograph is meaningless except insofar as it is a record of us in a place at a moment that is past.

The mind is many words at once, unlike photographs. Unlike poems.

The poem is this & not that, this word, not that. Like walking—one foot in front of the other—not like thinking.

No one can see me thinking about:

Or about:

Not the poem. Not the photograph.

The poem says "We" & means you. But not you & you, not *you*.

The poem is a bully. The poem is brutal. The poem is the present insofar as it was real/true/possible for one moment.

In the snapshot the Husband looks like my father, like my father looked a long time ago.
In the snapshot the Husband looks like a father. He is a father.

My mother has been gone a long time.
I look for her. I look like her.

All this water.

The poem says: "gone."

I have no eyes for this, I think, when the expanse of beauty is unremitting.

## FIVE MONTHS LATER I FINALLY
## HAVE SOMETHING TO SAY

to the poet who canceled on me when I invited you to visit my
class but your mother was ill & you had to fly to that city to see
her so we rescheduled & then you came to my class & my stu-
dents loved you,

I emailed you several times since asking were you all right by
which I meant was your mom OK & I think you said yes but I
don't remember. You seem OK. You're here now, aren't you?
About to give a lecture on color. Some of those same students
are here. You probably don't remember them but they loved
you. They loved you because you write funny poems & have
now written lectures. I am afraid to write either. But I'm here
too, aren't I? Maybe I'm all right? Maybe there are other reasons
they love you.

I saw you the semester after you visited my class, at a welcome
party at a place we both work. My mother had recently —  & I

could not stand up, but was. I could not teach, but had to. I did stand up. I was teaching. I was sure you knew what had happened, but you didn't say anything about it. I didn't say anything about it because I could not talk. Sometimes I had to say to myself: The way you know you are breathing is that you are thinking and if you weren't breathing you wouldn't be thinking. Mostly I had nothing to say to myself or anyone.

How are you? I said, at the welcome party. There were grilled shrimp but I wasn't eating them. What I meant was: I will never be myself, I am destroyed. I don't remember what you said. I felt invisible. Or you had no idea that my mother— I was inside what my mother had done/said & what had happened & no one could seem to— When I asked how you were you said you were terribly [adjective]. I can't remember which adjective because I was inside what my mother had done/said & what had happened. I was not myself.

My dog is sick, you said, Nothing is more terrible than a sick pet. I remember you said that, those words. Nothing is more terrible ... I remember you teared up. I think I'm not making this up, but I was not really there. I was inside something else, something that seemed more terrible. I wasn't sure though because

I was not sure of anything & because I have never loved animals so I thought perhaps I am not fully human. I remember thinking perhaps I lack some necessary understanding of life, some necessary understanding of what, in life, is most terrible.

That moment—the moment I did not care very much about your sick dog, when I found your tearful face affronting & the excitement of the students to see you destroying—was one of myriad (that's not the right word) bad-feeling moments I had at that time. That time when I felt I was looking up through the bottom of a glass-bottom boat at life, when I was looking at anything, when I even remembered the word for life which was not often. I didn't have the word "myriad" then. I call them "bad-feeling" moments but that's not right at all. I didn't have words for anything then. Or the words I had were wrong. I was so, so, so—"debilitrated" "aphased" "downded"—taken away.

I was can't-stand-up. I was can't-read can't-think can't-look-at can't-be-alone just time-to-time movies. Maybe if I ever loved animals, I thought, or had ever had a dog I loved, I would have had some comfort at that time which is still, if I am honest, this time, even though I do stand up, read, think, am alone & sometimes words. Part of that thick glass was jealousy. My students love you. Readers love you & I— My mother had not— It was a time & is a time— "I was not loved" was the color of— is the only way I can explain it.

Today, you're here to talk about color & poetry. I came to hear you. It is the day before the third big memorial which is the last, I hope, public performance of my grief & I needed to go away from making the slideshow of my mother young & old on a loop, the loop which is everywhere & anywhere & I cannot get away from, there is no where—

Yesterday Matt said, This is not grief anymore but turmoil. Or he said "torture" or maybe "torment." I can't remember. My memory is— My mind & all the words shot-through with the loop of her face old/young becoming my face.

You are talking about Plath & Stevens I think but I am always losing the train of your thinking. You joked just now about how I am sitting in the back by the door. You say I can leave if it goes on too long but you can go on for as long as you like because I am not listening to you. I am here to stop please pause the slide-show that is everywhere & always & I am in the back of the room writing you this note that I will never give you. It is either an apology or a thank you or neither, I can't remember.

What I have to say is that I didn't care that day about your dog & I'm sorry &/or thank you. This is one of myriad things I should never say to you or to anyone. I should never say I think there might be something more terrible than a sick pet but that is one of the few things I finally have to say. One of the few things I have finally found words for, the words to say. What I am trying to say is that I finally after all these months have something to say even though I should not say it, something less terrible than the things I have to say to my mother but can't, not because they are the most terrible which is to say unsayable but because she died.

# SOUNDMACHINE

When the manchild says, You're not listening, I am not listen-
ing.

Another time, when the manchild says, You're not listening, I
am. But it isn't the right kind of listening. It isn't a listening that
feels, to the manchild, like I am listening. He does not, as the
saying goes, *feel heard*.

When I ask the manchild to stop doing *x*, he does it again. Some
kind of clicking or ripping or fidgeting, a certain kind of lan-
guage or patting the head of babymanchild or one of the many
things babymanchild does not like the manchild to do that the
manchild does over & over & over. Stop, I say. The manchild
does it again. The way he looks at me as he does *x* again is called
"not-listening." It is also how I know he heard me.

Writing is a way of paying attention, I tell the students. They
continue doing *x*, which in this case is looking down at their

notebooks, which in this case tells me nothing about whether or not they're listening.

Sometimes, when the manchild speaks, I listen my brains out, listen with my whole heart. But it is not enough. I am the wire monkeymother with a bottle when he needs something soft & cloth-covered.

You're not listening, says the manchild again, sometimes just like that, in lowercase, more often with cursing & doorslamming.

The figurative bottle means nothing to the manchild; he is not hungry. Actually, he *is* hungry. He is always hungry but I never seem to have enough food or the right food. He has grown taller than I'll ever be & is ravenous.

Sometimes I listen as if my life depends on it, but all I hear is the silence after a doorslamming. It is the sound of the manchild not feeling heard.

Actually, it is not silence. It is a muffled tumult in the other room. It is the sound of not wanting to go after him. It is the sound of my body crossing the room, my hand on the doorknob.

Sometimes it is I who slam the door & then lie in bed listening to the sound of my own breathing & then my crying.

When the Husband says, It's hard to teach him not to slam the door when you slam the door, I think, How true. I listen to the sound of myself not slapping the Husband hard across the face. That is the sound of my breathing. The sound of the stare between us.

Do you have any questions? I ask the students. How are your dream journals going? How about the automatic writing? Well, I say, I guess this is the part of class when I ask questions and no one responds. OK, then, I say, Then we're all in agreement. Alrighty, I say. I can't believe I just said alrighty, I say.

On the way home I listen to a podcast about how the value of diamonds is held constant by limiting the number of diamonds entering circulation & convincing people not to sell the diamonds they already own. During World War II De Beers considered dumping a vault-load into the ocean as a way of staving off deflation.

Can you hear the sound of the white plate breaking in the sink? Can you hear the sound of my widened eyes? Or the text I send my friend: **I have become a person who breaks a plate in the sink.**

Sometimes, when the manchild speaks, I am listening to the sound of wanting to be elsewhere & the sound of myself thinking *stay* thinking *listen*, which sounds like the sound of the soundmachine over the Husband's snoring or perhaps the sound of snoring over the soundmachine, which is to say two sounds at once, which is to say hard to make sense of, which is to say *effortful*, which is to say a kind of listening unsatisfying to the manchild. Perhaps he wants my listening to look effort less which looks to him like love. Or perhaps he wants *more* effort?

On the subway two women scream at each other. One says, There is no more room, take the next train. The other says, You're taking up more than one space & presses into the crowded car. Everyone is listening intently to something on his headphones or has her eyes closed or pretends to be unaware of the two women, inches apart, screaming. Stop screaming, I scream above their screaming when I can no longer stand it. Don't talk to each other that way, I scream, my voice barely audible above their cursing. No one meets my eye. Trash, one yells. Get the fuck out of my face, the other yells. Stop shouting, I shout. No one can hear me.

The poem is what I listen to when listening to the city is just too much. The poem is a way of not paying attention. Of paying attention to the poem instead of. The poem is a soundmachine.

Uh-huh, I say to babymanchild as I walk him to school. He is either talking about Ellen DeGeneres or professional soccer. I am not listening. Sure, I say. OK, I say. I am not listening. I am still not listening.

Actually, I *am* listening. I am just not listening to him.

On the listserv which is everywhere & always I am accused of conflation. I am asked to be quiet. To listen. I am asked to read the offered links more carefully & to think about my behavior & the way in which asking the questions I've asked has caused people of color to perform labor on my behalf such as having to explain racism to me which is exhausting for them & a kind of white violence on my part. I am asked not to conflate race & gender. I am asked not to conflate the Confessional with Appropriation. I am asked not to conflate the Personal with the Conceptual. I am asked to understand that I will never understand, can never understand, what it is like to be other than who & what I am. I am asked to examine my privilege but quietly, to maybe think about why white people feel the need to take up all the space, why white people like me talk so much, use so many words. I am asked to listen more & talk less. I am asked to consider intersectionality.

You're not listening, says the manchild when he finds me reading & rereading the links.

On the subway some manchildren are jostling & joking & using language I don't want babymanchild to hear. I am trying to read to him but he isn't listening. He is listening to the manchildren, to the sound of his future. No, not *his* future for he will likely never speak like these manchildren. He is listening to the sound of his whiteness, which maybe for once is the sound of listening.

On the platform a man is lying on the ground, a wrapped granola bar inches away from his closed eyes. I can't get reception here, I say to babymanchild, pulling him away.

I want to ask the listserv about the difference between conflation & intersectionality, but I do not know how to ask this question while being quiet which I have been asked to be. I do not know how to listen more visibly, especially on a listserv where no one can see me reading the links & being quiet & sitting as still as possible, ignoring my children & waiting for someone to post something new for me to listen to. Somewhere on the list-serv: a doorslamming. More than one. I read & reread the links. The links tell me I am suffering from "white fragility." The links say I should listen.

Can you hear me? my friend asks, while reading me a new poem as I sit on the steps of a brownstone & shield the microphone from the sounds of the city. Yes, I say, I can hear you.

I lost you in the elevator, I say to another friend, whose mother is just home from the hospital & lives two blocks away from me & is very private & no, there is nothing I can do. When I ask if there is anything I can do for my friend who lives far from me & far from her mother just home from the hospital she says, Yeah, shoot me.

I call a third friend to read her this poem. She says, Take out the parts about the listserv—only the people on the listserv will understand those parts. Don't you know, I joke, that this poem is only for you? No one else will care about any parts. Also, she says, It's too long. I make it longer.

**I'm leaving**, the Husband texts. In this context it means he is coming home.

**I'm going to bed**, I respond, which means, in a way, I'm leaving.

The poem is a soundmachine. Whatever the family says they say over the sound of the soundmachine.

When babymanchild mentions Ellen DeGeneres or professional soccer as we walk to school I am relieved because this means I can think about other things & let his barely audible voice bleed into the city's ever-encroaching surround sound & in this way I am listening but this time to my own thoughts. Surely I am allowed from time to time such a luxury, am I not?

My thoughts, I'm thinking, are associational & interrupted just like my writing & I am probably thinking about my writing & about how a novelist friend once told me the secret was to not allow children to steal your muse time. She thought about her novels while watching her kids in the sandbox, while giving them baths, while putting them to sleep. Don't waste time wondering whether you have Cheerios in the pantry, she said to me, years ago. The relaying of this writerly advice to you is the length of time in real time it takes for babymanchild to yank my arm. His narrowed eyes & the line of his mouth accuse me. I am not listening.

Goodbye for now, I write to the listserv. I am tired of feeling wrong. Turns out I am not so good at listening, I write & I am tired of being wrong. After that I sit & listen to the virtual wall between their posts & me. I have turned off the listserv, which is still everywhere & always & all the other soundmachines whirring & whining.

The city is nothing if not conflation & believe me this city is not nothing. The city is a soundmachine.

When I read to babymanchild I listen to myself reading to babymanchild. Usually it sounds like childhood. Like a child who has a mother who listens even though it is actually the sound of a child listening to a mother reading. Actually, it is the sound of two people listening to a woman who long ago was writing to someone or no one.

The book requires explanation. We stop listening to the mother (me) reading & listen to the mother (me) explaining. Such as rape. Also racism, Hitler, violence against children & what Atticus means when he says: "There's nothing more sickening to me than a low-grade white man who'll take advantage of a Negro's ignorance. Don't fool yourselves—it's all adding up and one of these days we're going to pay the bill for it."

Perhaps all I am is conflation. What then? I would like to ask but can't ask it on the listserv because I've signed off.

When I have finished explaining everything in the world to babymanchild & have sat & held his hand until he's fallen asleep because it is hard to fall asleep when one's mother has just explained the worst of the world, I tiptoe from the room knowing that all this time I have not been listening to the manchild who has been waiting for me to come & listen. The manchild has been waiting to tell me that I am not listening, which is sometimes all he has to say.

Perhaps thinking is the soundmachine. The city is full of them. Faux rainforest, faux ocean. The jackhammer of it all. Whirring & churning until the death rattle.

A friend suggests nonviolent communication, suggests I cultivate silence. The listserv says nothing & cannot see me listening.

When the Husband & I speak to each other we hear things the other did not say. This may be because we are not listening. Or perhaps because we are listening too hard. Or listening wrongly. We break each other like plates in the sink. Other times the breaking is more like forgetting to water a plant for months at a time.

What?! he says when I have said nothing. Your *face*, he says, What?!

I didn't say anything, I say. Perhaps my face is the face of a person who is listening, trying to listen. Perhaps this is the problem. Everything we say sounds like disappointment & our silence is overfull of sorrow.

So sorry, I say when a woman bumps me on the subway. She looks at me with diamond-hard rage.

So, I say to the class, Can anyone tell me, what are some effects of addressing someone or something inanimate or absent in a poem? This is called apostrophe, I say. The poet brings the unreal closer, into the real, but the poem itself becomes a fictive space. I look at the real people around me who are saying nothing. During quiet writing I put them in the poem where they respond as readily as they do in real life.

Goodness, my friend says when an emergency vehicle passes by while I'm sitting on the steps of a brownstone, while she's reading me her long poem over the phone.

It's too long, the other friend says, when I read her this poem while she is in a hotel, alone, in Philly, when the poem is half as long as it is now.

Don't go, someone back-channels.

Good luck, another back-channels.

We will miss your voice.

My voice is all over the city.

Sometimes, at night, I beg the Husband to be quiet. I want his weight. Tell me, he asks, Just tell me what you want. What I want is no talking.

I am conflating again. Husband, manchild, babymanchild. Gender, sex, the personal, listserv.

I do not have Cheerios because no one in my family eats Cheerios. Otherwise I would have Cheerios. I am thinking about Cheerios. I am still thinking about Cheerios. If you said anything just now I was not listening.

In the crowded car I try to step carefully around a stroller so more people can enter the train. Stay there, I tell babymanchild. Hold the pole. No one helps him. The woman with the stroller glares at me.

I suspect that sometimes, when the manchild says I am not listening, he is not saying what he wants to say. He says & says & says & of course I am not listening because he wants me to hear something else, something he is not saying. The thing he is not saying underneath the thing he is saying. Sometimes I think I know what this might be. Other times I think there is no other thing, this is just a way of excusing myself for being a poor listener. Either way the sound of my own thinking takes up too much space in this family.

Stop, I say to the manchild. He keeps going. Isn't that what I want? Isn't the way he keeps going a sign of his resilience & of my maternal success? You're not listening, says the manchild. You're not listening. Stop talking, the world says to me. Stop talking, says the part of me who imagines the world is telling me to stop talking.

# NEED TO KNOW

I was speaking to the students & also to myself but no one in class had heard of Lenny Bruce & this made it difficult to explain anything to anyone.

At the reading, Rebecca Wolff said, That's how everyone talks to her lover or how lovers talk when their fingers are in each other's assholes. Brenda Shaughnessy said, I realized I was the cunty mother.

The students, who were also the audience, said, They didn't answer our questions!
One student said, You wouldn't call *your* mother cunty, would you?
Another said, No one ever wants to answer our questions!
Another said, Maybe we should just look at poems and not ask questions?

I didn't know what to say. I said, Maybe you just don't like hearing poems about middle-aged women having sex?

No one said anything.

One kind of time was moving so quickly. Another was slow & a third wasn't palpable except when I thought of my littlest son & felt [        ]. The Husband called & made a joke but nothing was funny. He said, So you're just done talking?

It was raining & I didn't want the little boy with me. It was raining & I wanted him with me. I was afraid he would be too heavy for me to carry when I got home. Maybe that wasn't what I was really afraid of.

I had breakfast with poet Cole Swensen who said things worth repeating or remembering but I don't remember so can't repeat them. What I remember Cole saying: J is ill—it came on fast. (Cole used J's full name of course.)

J probably *will* be angry with you, I remember Cole saying, And it's important not to hurt people so— Cole didn't finish the thought or maybe I just forget the end of her sentence, which was probably the most important part.

Rebecca Wolff was there & asked, What do you want to get out of all this? Or maybe I asked that & then tried to answer my own question. The question was whether or not to publish something that might hurt someone. "This" was either publishing or writing or life.

What's your question again? Rebecca asked.

Cole nodded & said, Tell us. Tell us what you really need to know.

# IN THE END

Start with a Yiddish curse or saying, says Erika, There are so many good ones. For example: *Shteyner zol zi hobn, nit keyn kinder*. She should have stones instead of children.

My son hears me say to Joan, on the phone, Today, no matter what, I *have to* write it.
Who's making you? my son asks.
No one, I say.
I don't understand, he says.

Snoekie, my grandmother's sister, used to say, We're not there yet.
She meant, we're not at the point of greatest difficulty, not at the moment when a decision is necessary.

What do you think will happen, when you show her the book? my therapist had asked.
She'll die, I had said.
I see, he had said.

I don't understand, my son says.

We're not there yet, Snoekie used to say.

She'll die.
How? Therapist Matt had asked.
A heart attack. Or a stroke. Or suicide.
Really? Matt had said.

*Tsen shifn mit gold zol zi farmogn, un dos gantse gelt zol zi fark-renkn.* She should possess ten ships of gold and spend all the money on medicine.

It's OK if it's difficult, I had said to Matt. But not if it's traumatic.

We are not there yet.

I had left them with their father. Had left my littlest one with his father whom he loved as much or more than he loved me, left him with a jar of 250 M&M's, ten for each of the twenty-five nights I would be gone.

I cannot write it in the living room because my son is practicing his new electric bass & saying, Look at this, look at this!

I cannot write it in the bedroom because that makes me need to lie down.

That summer I went to Paris I got on the plane & took an Ambien & a Xanax, which I'd never done before.

What am I worried about? I kept asking myself.

The book will *kill* her? Matt had said.
Yes, I had said.
And what if you don't show it to her?

Who is making you? my son asks.

I'd woken up, after three hours, sitting on the floor of the airplane, my head in my seat, my hand resting on the boot of the passenger sitting next to me. We were still at JFK, parked at the gate. There were mechanical difficulties & we would need to wait five hours for another plane. In a stupor, I gathered my things, got off the plane, spent the night on the floor of JFK watching an entire season of a TV show about a young wannabe writer & her friends living the sex-filled girlhood I'd never experienced.

I got sick but didn't die. I didn't even *almost* die, but I got sicker than I'd ever been & was sick for twenty out of the twenty-five days I was in Paris & then got sicker when I came home.

*A hiltsener tsung zol zi bakumen.* She should grow a wooden tongue.

It started as a bad cough, became a terrible cough, persistent & unremitting. I couldn't sleep, couldn't exercise—had to leave the room several times during each class, go out into the hallway & cough & cough, tears rolling down my face. I had to stop for several minutes on each landing of the four flights of stairs to my apartment on rue Vieille du Temple. I took each & any medicine the doctors & pharmacists offered. The whole thing had a nineteenth-century quality.

It was wonderful. I could eat or sleep when I wanted. Except I couldn't sleep & had little appetite. I watched movies on my laptop, listened to WNYC & watched the rain through the large French windows. I read a 900-page novel that took place over the course of three days. I spread the poems of my unfinished manuscript all over the table & all over the floor moving the pages around until I realized the order of the poems was not the problem & put them away.

I cooked two meals a day & drank codeine cough medicine & inhaled steroids. I went to readings & out to dinner every other night. I walked slowly from arrondissement to arrondissement, stopping to catch my breath, tears running down my cheeks after each coughing fit. I went to a handsome French doctor who was unimpressed by my symptoms but gave me more medicine.

*Verter zol men vegn un nit tseyln.* One should weigh words, not count them.

I played Candy Land over Skype—Judah flipping our cards for both of us & moving our pieces. You *never* win, he cried, when I won. I couldn't explain that at home I cheated to lose. Another time he performed a puppet show for me but the puppets kept wandering out of the camera's range & all I could see was the bookshelf behind him, Judah saying "I *kill* you . . . no, I kill *you* . . ." Every time we spoke he asked why I'd gone to Paris, which he pronounced "perish."

*Ir vort zol zayn a shtekn, volt men zikh nisht getort onshparn.* If her word were a stick, you couldn't lean on it.

I went to the market & came home with two bags of groceries including eight perfect peaches. I didn't know how to shop for one person. I didn't know how to think for one person. I couldn't believe how long the days seemed, how luxurious it was to be sick but not have to take care of anyone but myself. At night I sat up, sleepless & coughing, terrified of every sound.

A student wrote a poem that mentioned Adolf Hitler & another student ran crying from the room. Why would he do that? a third student asked, Why would anyone write something that would hurt other people? I asked the class if they'd heard of Lenny Bruce.

I gave a reading with other faculty & sipped hot tea with honey. I read a poem in which I quoted something from a friend's email, something he'd written that had hurt my feelings. I used the friend's first initial.

I learned to buy two peaches at a time. I learned to buy one. I stopped buying the foods my children loved that I hated such as melons, tomatoes, raspberries & croissants.

"A mother traveling without her children is everywhere a woman in a foreign country," I'd written in a poem ten years earlier.

"I was never a girl // never but mother never," I'd written in a poem five years earlier.

I watched movies & walked all over town to find miso soup mix. I ate fruit & drank miso soup. I read the crazy-long novel. I coughed & gagged & began to hear a whoop.

"I am becoming someone else," I wrote in my notebook. "I am taking off the self I've put on, piece by piece, child after child."

I cannot write this in the kitchen because the beans have been cooking for three hours & if I go into the kitchen I will have to sauté onions, garlic, cumin & oregano in olive oil.

*Ir vort zol zayn a brik, volt ikh moyre gehat aribertsugeyn.* If her word were a bridge I would be afraid to cross it.

"If I'm not the mother who stays, who am I?" I wrote four years ago.

My friend was furious with me for quoting his email in my poem, for reading the poem in public, in front of him. He shouted at me & I cried. He berated me for crying. Something is wrong with you, he said. You made me look like a cunt, he said.

Something *was* wrong with me.

Who is making you? my son asks.

She did not die. I did not die.

I went out for coffee with Alice Notley. Cole Swensen went with me & we walked together from the old Jewish quarter to meet Alice at her favorite café in the ninth arrondissement. I'd told Cole about my manuscript & she encouraged me to talk to Alice.

*Shtek nit dem kop tsum volf in moyl arayn.* Don't stick your head in a wolf's mouth.

We are not there yet as Snoekie always said, my father often says.

Send it to me when it comes out! Alice said, waving away my offer to let her read it before it was published. Your mother and I had the same haircutter in the East Village, Alice said, Alice had two *cafés*. I had a *citron pressé*.

When I came home I got sicker. We went to Denver to see Josh's mother & in the middle of the night I woke up with a pain in my chest so bad I couldn't sit or lie down. I stood, holding on to the side of the bed, trying not to cough because when I coughed it felt like something was breaking.

*Mit a lefl ken men dem yam nit oys'shepn.* You can't empty the ocean with a spoon.

I can't write this in the bathroom.

The urgent care doctor looked at my chest X-ray & said, I won't even tell you what I was looking for.

I know what you were looking for, I said.

Anyway, it's whooping cough and you've broken a rib, blown out an eardrum and burst several blood vessels at the back of your throat.

I'd wanted to keep a little distance from the children, just a little—what the French call a *soupçon* (a taste, a trace)—a little sense of what it felt like to be a not-mother in Paris. But what followed were days of lying in bed in my mother-in-law's house, knocked out on muscle relaxants & jacked up on albuterol. I didn't feel like anyone's mother. Didn't feel like anyone.

I didn't die & she didn't die, I thought, lying in bed, trying not to cough.

I wrote to Jorie, but she didn't write back.

Peeka says, Your mother had a karmic responsibility to you that she could not fulfill. You have one to your children but not to her. That's how it works.

*Oyskrenkn zol zi dos mame's milkh.* She should get so sick as to cough up her mother's milk.

When I think of my angry writer-friend, years later, I still feel ashamed & that is but one of my lesser sins.

*An eyzl derkent men in di lange oyern, a nar in der langer tsung.* An ass is recognized by the long ears, a fool by the long tongue.

I can't write this in the playground. Come here! my son calls. Come NOW!

She had wanted to know why I kept writing about suicide. She said, I understand I wasn't there for you and that was extremely painful. She said she had done the best she could but she knew it wasn't good enough. She said she was sorry. She wanted to talk about the divorce. About her sex life with my father. About the years when all she could do was try not to cry in front of me. She asked if my father had bought my love, was that why I loved him? She wanted to know why I hadn't told her all these things directly but had written about it instead. She wanted to know if I'd been abused as a child, maybe by a babysitter or by my babysitter's teenage sons. She wanted to know, if I had not been abused, why I refused as an adult to have a relationship with my babysitter, why I made a face every time my baby-sitter's name was mentioned. She said I hadn't told the whole story. She said there were things I'd gotten wrong, so many things. She wanted to talk about her affair. Next Monday? Next Tuesday? Next week?

Lung problems are usually the site of stored grief, said the acu-puncturist. She inserted the smallest, thinnest needles & I cried out.

She had wanted me to know she'd given the book to four friends & described it to a fifth. The first friend had said the book wasn't true. The friend knew because she'd been there & lived through all of this with us. The second friend said the book could have been great if it had been written differently. The third said I was clearly in a lot of pain. The fourth friend said he almost couldn't read it because it was unremitting whining without a single redemptive quality.

I imagined cancer growing somewhere in my body.

*Di pen shist erger fun a fayl.* The pen stings worse than an arrow.

I cannot write this in a coffee shop. Not on a plane, not in a car, not on a train, says Dr. Seuss.

*Ab initio mundi* means "from the beginning of the world."

I feel like I need to write something about what happened and put it at the end of the book, I said to Katy.

Don't put that at the end, Katy said, It will overdetermine everything that came before.

Why can't you say that's not all there is? my mother had asked. I did, I said. I did say that.

*Ab ovo usque ad mala from the egg to the apples* (Horace, Satire 1.3) means "from beginning to end," based on the main Roman meal, which typically began with an egg dish & ended with fruit (cf. the English phrase *soup to nuts*).

I cannot write this without a word that means "when the end is the beginning" but I cannot find that word.

The way birth is the end of pregnancy & the beginning of motherhood.

Thus *ab ovo* means "from the beginning."

Commencement is close but not quite right.

You got so many things wrong, my mother had said.

I told you stories every other night, she had said. Not only your father.
I don't remember that, I had said.

It wasn't my mother who called me when my father died, it was my mother's maid, my mother had said. You were always the most important thing, my mother had said. Until you were seven we were very close, my mother had said.

In Hebrew, the word *emet* or "truth" is one of the names of God. It is made up of the first, middle & last letters of the alphabet, implying that truth is reached (or sought) in completeness, in all the letters & all the words.

The Hebrew word for "end," *sof*, begins with the letter *samekh*, one of only two closed letters in the alphabet. It looks like a circle. The end is at the beginning. The end is when you come back.

She didn't die.

Then she did.

Years ago the poet Kristin Prevallet came to my class to talk about her book *I, An Afterlife*, in which she tells the story of her father's suicide.

Other languages don't have a word for "closure," Kristin said, And therefore no expectation that something like closure should or can exist, especially in relation to an emotional state like grief.

Memoirs are famously hard to let go of, Katy had said. Are you sure you're not just having trouble letting go?

We were not talking about *this* book, which of course I hadn't written yet.

Did die.

And when my mother did, I became the only she.

It took a long time for the urn to arrive from Taiwan. I wanted to send some of the ashes to Bernard, her old boyfriend, so he could bury them in the South of France in the cemetery where Bernard's father was buried, a cemetery my mother had said she liked in a very old document on her computer that I was only able to access when the computer was returned to me from Taiwan & the document was decoded by my friend Dan. I wanted to bury some in her garden before the landlord made me return the keys to her emptied-out, rent-controlled apartment where I'd grown up. But I was afraid to open the urn. The Husband was afraid. He worried there would be lasting damage brought on by touching a parent's ashes.

*Vi tsu derleb ikh zi shoyn tsu bagrobn.* I should outlive her long enough to bury her.

David Daniel Kaminsky (Danny Kaye) said, No one has the right to write about me because no one knows me.

"She was glad that the cosy house, and Pa and Ma and the firelight and the music, were now. They could not be forgotten, she thought, because now is now. It can never be a long time ago," wrote Laura Ingalls Wilder at the end of *Little House in the Big Woods*, the first in the Little House on the Prairie series.

You know that's fiction, right? said Laurel.

One winter day—two winters after she died—I was walking home wearing a long coat that I had bought with money I had inherited from her, pushing a full cart of groceries into the frigid wind. I suddenly felt old. Older than I'd ever felt & when I looked down: those were my mother's hands on the metal handle. Not my hands that look like hers. *Her hands.*

*In di zumerdike teg zol zi zitsn shive, un in di vinterdike nekht zikh raysn af di tseyn.* On summer days she should mourn & on wintry nights she should pull out her teeth.

On the first full day of the women's group, Peeka says, Walk anywhere you want until something speaks to you, calls you.

Look at it, observe it. Ask yourself, What are its qualities? Ask yourself what qualities you have that reside in this object.

I walk down the shady path toward the river. Two deer—a mother & fawn—appear & I am afraid. I am afraid of the deer & of the cool path, afraid of entering a fairy tale. I turn away, walk back toward Peeka's house & garden.

After my mother died my youngest son began to look more & more like her. His eyes, his coloring, his slender body & lithe movements. When I mentioned this, people would say, I was afraid to say anything to you—it's uncanny. I wondered if you'd noticed, people would say.

One woman wants to choose valerian, another rue or roses. I want poppies for vision & comfort & the third woman agrees. But Peeka made a deal with the poppies—if they grew she would not cut them for the first four years—so we cut bud after yellow bud of rue for a flower essence that each of us will use as our intuition instructs.

I am afraid to not be afraid, I say, when Peeka tells us rue is good for overcoming fear. Like how the pain of labor reminds you to move around & without it—I try but cannot explain.

118

Forget everything you know about the flower, says Peeka. Forget its story. Just *feel* it.

A Jewish burial home nearby had agreed to divide the ashes into three separate parcels. I sent one to France & took another down to Greenwich Village, to the garden she'd tended for more than forty years, that I would never have access to again. Josh & the older boys looked at me in horror as we sat around the metal table & I spoke about my mother. My youngest son, five at the time, was sitting in my lap & had opened the box. Was touching what was inside.

I would not describe them as ashes. The larger bone fragments looked like coral. The rest like petrified wood.

Peeka had asked us each for our date & time of birth so she could do our star charts, but my birth certificate said only "baby girl Wolkstein" & the date. There is no one living who remembers what time of day or night I was born.

Like how birth is the end of pregnancy & the beginning of motherhood if the baby lives which I did.

*A patsh farheylt zikh, a vort gedenkt zikh.* A slap heals, a word remembers.

One woman sits cross-legged on the stone patio, looking at a clump of yarrow & writing in her notebook. A second sits in the shade of the shed. A third is nowhere in sight. I stand in the garden feeling stupid, hating the smell of the roses, afraid to step on something precious. A string of rusted chimes hangs from the rose-choked trellis, a yellowed bar-code sticker curling off the largest bell. A wooden pistil dangles in each upside-down metal cup, but there is no wind to move them.

"The birds and insects make the silence of the chimes audible," I write.

"Does sound come from the stick hitting its own cup or from the cups hitting each other?" I write.

"For want of wind," I write.

"Difference b/w capacity and ability?" I write.

"Why not touch them?" I write. I do not touch them.

"For want of a living garden," I write.

"Unlike the cups, the chain is not rusted—what protects it (the spine?) from the elements?" I write.

Snoekie was just barely strong enough to hold my firstborn son, three days old, her great-grandnephew—I held her as she held him—& three days later (the last of my grandparents' living siblings) died.

Stay in the unknowing, Peeka says. We nod. I have no idea what she means. Perhaps the other women know. I am afraid to ask them. We pass the crystal & speak, in turn, about anything, for as long as we want.

My grandmother, Sheindel, later Charlotte, more often Lotty, daughter of a Polish-born, Antwerp-based diamond dealer, spoke Yiddish, sometimes French, to my grandfather as she peeled apples for me, after school. She made one long continuous peel as we sat on the long couch of her apartment on the Upper West Side, which is the neighborhood I live in now. She's no longer alive. I was a child then & played the smallest sized violin, which my grandfather saved in case I would one day be famous.

How can I explain?

The crystal in my hands is neither cool nor warm. It is smooth
& clear with a streak of white, like a scrim of clouds, running
through it.

I hold the crystal & close my eyes. I see the rusted chimes. I say,
I was made to make a sound.

# CONFESSIONAL

This afternoon I've got a meeting with ____ ____ to tell her that
the poem in which I call her my ____ ____ has been destroyed
& I'll never publish it or read it at a reading because I'm done
writing about anyone I work with, she has my word.

In a lecture I wrote, I say I've been influenced by photography
more than poetry & spent years writing poems in response to
photography's characteristic concerns. I say my career in poetry
is one long synesthetic mistake. Now you can skip the lecture
that anyway you weren't planning on attending. Also, the lec-
ture's not really about photography & this isn't a poem.

My new friend Monica just texted me. I'm allowed to use her
name because she's not a poet & I don't work with her & I have
n't yet made that promise to ____ ____. Monica's very
beautiful & intimidating & I like her because, even though we
haven't ____ ____ together, we admitted to each other in low
voices, in the dry goods aisle of Whole Foods, that we each like
to ___ ____. I don't remember how the topic came up & can't

say what Monica & I like because we're moms & it's not legal so I shoot blanks to protect her.

In my second lecture, the one about the legacy of confessional poetry, I get into it with Anne Sexton who is a terrible mother but a better poet than most people think. I talk about Lowell, Plath, Snodgrass but not so much Berryman. In the end, the lecture's mostly me looking at Sexton looking at Sexton & at her daughter & her mother who are also Sexton.

Sexton, as I said, is a very good poet & a very bad mother. I say "is" because mothers can be bad even if they're dead. My mother is. Bad & dead.

"As if it were normal / to be a mother and be gone," wrote Sexton.

Meanwhile _____'s mother has _____ which is sad & she would not like anyone to know.

I've got a poetry reading tomorrow with _____ & _____ who are excellent poets & intimidate me. Also, I love them & they are generous & by generous I mean not easily offended, which is a kind of love, don't you agree?

I don't know what to read. I'm sick of that new poem about my son worrying about death & the photographer Sally Mann & _____ has heard that already. I could read the poem about _____'s death, the one in which I use people's initials instead of names so as not to offend them but _____'s brother suggested I change the initials to different initials & I haven't done that yet.

An editor, by which I mean ____ _____, suggested I take the names out of my book. Can't you do the same thing without using names? he asked. So I took out the name of a famous poet I didn't know but kept dreaming about. The poems were kinder then or maybe crueler. They were definitely not the same. They were more about me & not about what had happened to the poet's daughter.

I wonder, I said to the editor, If naming is a kind of love? But the editor said, Hasn't he suffered enough? Tell them about the time you took out the names and it made the poem better, says the editor.

Lowell's poems were a "ghoulish operation on his soul" said M. L. Rosenthal & Adrienne Rich called Lowell's disclosures "bullshit eloquence," I said in a lecture.

If you don't have anything nice to say don't say anything, says everyone.

I say nothing for five minutes. Then I say, By the way I was paid $_____ to write the lectures but it's *gauche*—pardon my French—to discuss money.

Just then _____ calls. I say, You really don't want to talk to me right now. She could hear tears in my voice & said, What's up? I told her I'd been rejected from _____ & _____ & would not be spending any weeks writing in the woods waiting for a covered basket of lunch. Also I did not get a _____ & I had not been invited back to teach at _____.

All that's not real! she shouted, which is something _____ never does, You get everything! Even the *New Yorker*! I wanted to hang up I felt so _____ but I knew she was right, this was not real. I felt _____ & _____, which felt all too real. Later _____ would apologize & say she was not herself but she *was* herself & I knew I should feel _____ of myself.

I mean really, what is it I don't have that I want? I ask myself. That's the wrong question says _____.

If this is not a poem can I read it tomorrow at the reading?

If this is not a poem what is it?

A way to spend time with me?

A way for me to waste your time?

We voyeur each other & I perversify my proclivity to unprevaricate.

_____ will not like the way I disparage myself in this way. _____ will not like the way I am clearly talking about _____ & _____ & _____ & what will the gay guys think?

Does it offend everyone equally? asks _____.

Does that make it all right, I ask?

Without seeing the poem I have no way to know, says _____ but _____ doesn't have time to read the poem or hear it on the phone.

Without the poem I have nothing to show of myself, I say.

Do you mean "for yourself"? _____ asks.

I have nothing other than these lectures. (I almost wrote "which cost me my right arm," but didn't write that because that's not true although writing them has felt like _____ & has been hard as shit & fucked up my language, which is why I just wrote "hard as shit," which is a stupid thing to write. At the very least I should write "hard as old shit" since fresh shit isn't hard at all. "Hard as old shit" is more precise but is not something a real poet writes in a real poem.)

I write: "My son is very boring. To be more precise, I find being with him boring."

He wants to talk about soccer or Star Wars or Ellen DeGeneres, none of which interests me. I did, however, like the new Avengers movie because Mark Ruffalo & Robert Downey Jr. are hot as hell or hot as shit or hot as ____. I'm allowed to name them in poems because they're celebrities & also this is not a poem.

> *just write "often"*
> *just write "like"*
> *just write "the way the light [dot] [dot] [dot]"*
> *say "landscape" or say nothing*

For the record I, too, am a bad mother. Actually, I am an amazing mother, but all I want to do is work.

The other two sons are not boring. To be more precise, I find being with them enormously stressful.

*I sometimes often find the way the light the landscape.* Haha.

All I want to do is work.

"Perverse" as in: a deliberate, obstinate desire to behave in a way that is unacceptable.
As in· T minus minutes to soccer.
Or: roll two sheets of paper together—black & any other color—tape the seam = makeshift light saber.

The most interesting thing about me is _____.

That last blank has been left blank not because I am afraid of hurting someone's feelings or that it will negatively affect my career but because there is nothing interesting about me. If I were not practicing discretion I'd say the only interesting thing about me is my compulsive confessing.

Dear Anne Sexton
you were a bad mother

I am a better mother
than you were
bully for me
that's not saying much
on the other hand
you are a better poet
so many are this is not
false modesty
this is the truth
which no one
asked me for

After hearing my lecture on photography, Colin said I could not
use the word "truth" without indexifying the term. I have no
idea what Colin means & here I use his real name as a way of
calling him out & to protect myself from the shame of believing
in truth. If I can't say "truth," fuck it, I'll write "Colin" even if he
is the boyfriend of my dear friend & might not like being in this
poem. There I go again calling everything a poem!

I'm sick of my "I" & "she" pronouns, sick of what an editor called
"the role of authenticity in your work" in which "role" means
pretending something is something else, in which "you" means
I. For example I am not actually sick when I say being a woman

is \_\_\_\_\_ to me all these babies later. When I say being straight & white *wah wah* [dot] [dot] [dot]

It is despicable to be so _____. I mean really it is \_\_\_\_\_ to be so _____.

After my lecture on the legacy of confessional poetry my fifteen-year-old son said, So your lecture's about how we should feel sad for unhappy white women which you are? Everyone laughed. My son is very funny & smart. Not often hardly boring.

It turns out my sons are my best work but all I want to do is work.

Put it in the book! says \_\_\_\_, about a book we are & are not writing together, a sequel to our book about birth. This one will be about sex & middle age & we will say all the things we did not say before which will be very difficult to do after I make my vow. Oh me & my upcoming meeting! Will \_\_\_\_ \_\_\_\_\_ believe I've seen the error of my ways? Not if she comes to this reading.

What I want is a socially acceptable financially viable reason to be away from my children for weeks & weeks & weeks & weeks.

Last night I dreamed I was trying to get the Husband to have sex with me & every time he acquiesced it turned out we were in public. Despite the fact that no one seemed interested in watching us, he kept stopping because he was not into having sex in public & we ended up (in the dream) watching a movie with ____ & ____ & ____ put his hand on my leg & it occurred to me that this might be what I'd long ago experienced as a come-on although even in the dream the phrase "come-on" was so remote I kept thinking it wasn't the right idiom. Meanwhile, ____ had his hand on my leg & I thought (in the dream) at this point there is *no way* I would say no to *anyone*, which is not the same exactly as wanting to say yes to ____, but looks a lot like it because of course ____ *is* "anyone."

____, who shouted at me because I get everything even the *New Yorker* & with whom I am & am not writing a book, has ____ sex. She has it a lot & writes about it. I know this because she tells me all about it. Actually she tells me as much as she thinks I can handle, which is not very much. Also, I just read her new book which was supposed to be about her dead baby but has an awful lot of sex in it none of which is awful. In fact, I just read her poem about a student she had a crush on & how she wondered if her instructions in workshop were a kind of come-on which reminded me of my dream & also of my vow never to write a poem like that again at least not after my meeting which is in only a few hours. From now on I will only write about Mark Ruffalo & Robert Downey Jr. & I will not listen to my friend when she says if I want my needs met maybe I need a new partner so there we are:

Me & my _____ friend & her ___ poems & mine, although this is not a poem.

Dear Mom
I wrote two lectures
one about photography
& one about confessional
poetry but they were not
about those things
both lectures were
veiled ways of
explaining to you
why I insisted on
publishing a book
you didn't want me
to publish
it is difficult to
explain this to you

because you are
dead because you died &
the last thing you said
to your therapist was
"Tell Rachel not to
publish the book"
& I did anyway
I thought Dad had
lost his mind
when he said
"I *am* upset
Diane died—this
makes it much more
difficult to speak
with her."
I called my
stepmother to say
please deal with
Dad I couldn't
deal with anything
not myself not my
sons I had become
a woman who had

killed her own
mother but Dad
was right it *is*
more difficult
to speak to you
but I keep trying


Dear Mom
I think I have to
write the story of
what happened
this time without
research without
indexifying anything
if I even knew what
that meant I think
I will never be able
to write a poem
until I can
explain myself
to you which I
never can

Perhaps that's why I'm stupid enough to swear I'll never write another poem about anyone I know or use names, only my own maybe not even my own even if it means I show up to the reading with nothing new nothing mine nothing "true."

I almost wrote love cancer Wayne Jason Arielle 40K Yaddo Mac-Dowell Guggenheim Daniel enraged ashamed exposed torture elitist crazy obnoxious privilege narcissistic libidinous lusty but stopped myself just in time.

# PLANET HULK

When I opened my eyes, people showed me the footage: there
I was destroying the city.
A bystander went down. A citizen, an onlooker.

Or there was no footage, the footage was my own mind.
My hand around her tiny throat: the power of it, the clarity, be-
fore nothing made sense.

Was I, I asked, Really that bad?
No, said one Avenger, We love you.
No, said an X-Man, You are what you are.
No, said Natasha, I needed you.

I lied. They averted their eyes.
Yes, *that* bad, they all said. Of course they did.

The lullaby's working, Natasha says, as I become small, weak,
feminine. As I come to & grope for my glasses.

The editor says, You made an image of me at one moment in time, reductive like all photography, it is not even an image of me just your projection of me and it subjectifies.

Will it help if I add that to the poem? If I say, "you are not you, you are my projection of you"?

I speak wearing the wounded look of Mark Ruffalo playing Bruce Banner, a look that often reads as false. And who would like to play the role this time of my rejecting mother? You? You? Step right up I'll play the daughter & kill you. I take names in vain until I'm made of vanity. Would you like to see me *really* angry?

When I opened my eyes, I saw excitement on all the wrong people's faces. These were the people who loved me.

Wow, says Laurel, Great poem.
I love it, says the Husband.

Whatever was wrong with me was wrong with Laurel, with the Husband, with the people who shared my perversity, which was indistinguishable from my poetry.

You have a triangulated reality-writing-shame fetish, Katy said. The fetish might be a kind of edging, someone said.

O You whom I've exposed, I've stood before you tone deaf & prurient & asked you to love me.

When I opened my eyes Marina Abramović had carved a star into my stomach & my face felt slapped a thousand times, my back raw with lashes. I was seared & blistered by the gaze of a live camera. Or it was footage of *me* slapping *you*, some of you liking it. Some of you just onlookers, caught in the crossfire.

There were casualties. It was unbecoming. But was also *me*. For in this way & only in this way was I furthermore alive.

Change the ending, Katy said, Also, the names make it less interesting.

It's not *that* bad, another friend said, You're taking yourself too seriously.

When I opened my eyes Sylvia Plath was making small cuts on my upper arm with a boning knife. It will hardly show, Plath whispered. This isn't my thing, I said, trying to pull away, but Plath's eye is inescapable.

There's a fine line between self-flagellation and bragging, Katy chides.

No poets were harmed in the making of this poem. Do you believe that? Then stop reading. I cover myself in bright blood like a flag.

So many things were given unto me that I took as givens. My sex, my gender, my race, my class—I never sought to question. I was born into & became more & more my cis. Cis this, cis that, as if life were simply a matter of seeing oneself more & more in focus, as if "truth" were a word an "I" like me could use.

Maggie Nelson, could you come kill Sylvia Plath before she does herself in again, before no one can escape her wrath—I mean wraith?

No one will know who Maggie Nelson is, Katy says.

Everyone knows who Maggie Nelson is, Laurel says.

Eventually the Avengers send Hulk away because even Veronica (Hulk's self-created fail-safe self-destruct creation) cannot contain him, nor can his homo-hero friends. Hulk is a weapon too dangerous to possess so they trick him onto a spaceship & shoot him into the sky.

Banner always falls for feeling needed but it's always Hulk they need. Gamma gamma everywhere but not a drop to drink. My shame is a tsunami; it's time to get up & make breakfast.

David Trinidad suggests I wear a black tourmaline for protection. It repels negative energy, he tells me, which is important when reading poems about people when those people are present and the poems might upset them.

Or you could stop writing those kinds of poems, someone sensible suggests.
Or you could stop caring about hurting people, someone who wishes to remain anonymous says.

What if I can't "get off" without hurting someone? I ask Arielle, In the poem I mean. Everyone knows I am, otherwise, outside poems, rather nice, always on time, considerate, so what? What if there is no "I" outside these poems?

By day I was Penelope waiting & weaving. By night I was Penelope, waiting & weaving but Hulk too also I—

It's our sun that gives Superman his extraordinary powers. The shards of his exploded planet & pieces of his past & home enfeeble him which is to say *humanize* which is to say see how it hurts to feel, to be human? Hulk, a universe away, is less lucky. Hulk is made of anger of animal & is always human. In some versions Hulk rarely hurts anyone innocent. In other versions, he's just a monster.

When I opened my eyes, I saw footage of my youngest son saying *I love you so much*. It is a crack in the Earth's core & I would throw my body into the molten to stop it up but my body is not enough.

When he says I love you he means he is afraid beyond reason or measure & more than words can wield the matter. There is nothing to save him from this fear. It is eclipse & kryptonite. It is the pain of being mortal with a mortal mother. He is exactly old enough to suspect what my absence would look like.

When he says *I love you* so *much* he means: I cannot yet survive you dying. And I called this "boring"? I barely survive his fear which is his love. His weakness makes him hate me & this is his love.

This is art not a court document, someone reminds me.

Poems are the agency of desire in a world of diverse subjectivities, Laurel says.

Put this in a drawer for at least three months and don't look at it even for a moment, then revise.

No, says another, Keep going with your noble enterprise of telling the truth in arresting forms.


Banner always falls for being needed, but it's always Hulk they need. Don't feel bad for Banner. He brought this on himself. Not even a mutant, just too ambitious. I make the Husband sleep in the other room. We have bodies & mine is keeping him awake, the tender laptop-tapping of my massive fingers.


A famous poet writes "perp" in the margins of her drafts, meaning she's a perp, meaning this poem must be sealed for perpetuity which in this case is thirty years after anyone mentioned in the poem has died.


Every description of anything is reductive, says Laurel, That's the limit of language. The editor is saying what your mother said which is "This isn't the way I understood it. This isn't how I remember things," says Laurel, But that doesn't mean your story isn't true or that you don't have a right to tell it.

Does Alice Notley worry? I wonder. Did Frank O'Hara?

In the Secret Wars storyline, 2015, Hulk discovers a secret place called Greenland filled with hundreds of Hulks. I'm sure Lowell is there & Plath & Sexton & all the scapegrace barbarians.

I would put my hand on your back, says Laurel, But I don't know how else to make you feel better. No, I say, Take me to Greenland so we can destroy each other & make poetry safe for the civilians.

## AFTER THE NEW COUPLES THERAPIST OR "TO SPEAK OF WOE THAT IS IN MARRIAGE"

Is it going to be a problem, you said, If I pass out after reading this article about Trump?

Well, I said, Why don't you spend the time you would have spent with Trump with me instead and then pass out? which was we both knew almost the same as saying, "we're alone in the apartment would you consider fucking me?" Almost, but not quite the same as saying that.

You got into bed, positioning your pillows while scrolling & swiping. I said, I know you're less interested in me than in Trump or Sanders because they're so obviously exasperating, but where do I stand in relation to Hillary, you know, interest-level-wise? which was almost the same as saying "please stop looking at that racist fuckwad and that finger-wagging old man on your phone and fuck me"—almost the same, but not quite.

You said, Well, you're exasperating too & smiled, put the phone down & closed your eyes.

Just so you know, I said, The Philosopher emailed me an MV4 this morning. I only heard the first few sentences, didn't have time to listen to the rest. Guess I'll listen now it's about a dream he had—

M4V is a movie, you said, He sent you a movie?

M4A, I said. Or whatever, I said. It's a sound file of him telling me about a dream he had, I guess about me?

You opened your eyes. And was this, you asked, Before or after you *you know* and then couldn't sleep all night last night? Your eyes closed again.

After, I said. Or, who knows, maybe before? Maybe he was having his dream *while* I was *you know*. I turned on my side & wondered if you were looking at the space between the bottom of my T-shirt & the top of my tight jeans that were giving me a backache. Rolling over like that was almost the same as saying "put your hand on my ass, put your hand on my ass, put your hand for fuck's sake on my ass." Almost, but not quite.

I'm so glad you're jealous, I said.

I'm not jealous, you said, That guy's a freak.

He's a *philosopher*, I said, which was almost the same, we both knew, as saying, "I still remember how he, that he, how he …"

Whatever, you said, putting in your sound-canceling head-phones.

Fine, I said, putting in my earbuds which was almost the same as saying "I'm going to listen to the voice of a man who twenty-three years ago, but who's counting … I'm going to put these small white buds in my ears & listen to the voice of a man … I'm going to let his voice into me, even though I do not know what he is going to say only that he starts out: *Rachel I just had this dream it ended … with me … running into you …*" which is almost the same as a man saying "I remember what you re-member twenty-three, but who's counting, years later … I re-member you & the dim light, what it felt like …" Almost like that, but not quite.

Whatever he was going to say, I was going to let him. Unless you—which was almost the same as saying "do anything …

something ... call for a contested election." Instead, your breathing became regular & rote while the Philosopher's voice said & said, this & that, the dream went here & there. It was a big audio file.

The Philosopher said: *you were sitting at the bar looking bemused ... seeing you was like seeing ... an old friend ... that was the feeling I had when I saw you. You said hey how's it going? and I suddenly just told you ... I told you what I was actually feeling ...*

The Philosopher's voice was full of sleep. What was he trying to tell me? He said: *in the dream you leaned in ... and with my head, I put it ... on your shoulder ... it was a gesture of ... and I said I'm tired of this ... it's been a long time to be out here ... I meant a long time to be out in the water, out at sea, away from shore ...*

By then you were snoring. No one was touching my anything, or talking to me, except the Philosopher whose voice went on & on inside my ears.

The Philosopher said: *you'd just had an argument like you talk about in some of your poems with Josh but you guys were made*

*up and happy and it was just part of your normal life ... there*
*was a sense of you as a person who had figured out how to get*
*through things in life ... The feeling I had ... I thought you should*
*know ... you were a person who exuded a kind of ... you were*
*someone I could say something like that to ... you just ... when*
*I looked at you ... you were—*

He called me *motherly?!* I said aloud. You didn't move. Guy fuck-
ing called me *motherly,* I muttered, which is the same as saying
"it's a long time to be swimming . . . a long time to be so far from
shore." Or was it more like saying, "it's a long time to be stuck
on shore"? I didn't know anymore.

All too soon it was time for Hebrew school pickup, dinner & back
home so sad-sack son could write a paper on *Invisible Man* while
the other one played the same song over & over, each time
louder. I finally found the tincture that doesn't do anything to
put on the little boy's wart & answered emails [not the Philos-
opher's] until it was still somehow early enough to—even after
reading/brushing/flossing goodnight & goodnight & "turn out
that light" "turn down, actually turn *off* the music" "pick a pas-
sage in the book that didn't get discussed in class or a quote
you loved—really you didn't underline *anything*?"—back in bed
together—

How? you asked, Are we ever going to have sex again? which was, we both knew, a cry for help, or simply a way of asking "do you want to?"

Are you gun shy? I asked, which was almost the same as saying "there's almost nothing you could do to fuck this up other than do nothing." But how could you know that, how could you not know? Which was almost like saying "yes" to a question you hadn't quite asked.

I'm locking the door, you said.

I said absolutely nothing, which was my way of saying "stop talking," which I had said so many times before, even in poems. We'd said enough for one day, a week, maybe forever.

I honestly don't know, I'd said, when that therapist had asked, And what's been going on that made you, as you say, *almost break up?*

You'd said, It's not just the snoring, when the therapist had asked about our separate beds.

I don't want to break up, I'd said, But don't want to be this un-happy either, which was almost the same as saying what I didn't have words for, still don't.

You finally, after all, touched me, which was almost the same as not saying anything, which was what I wanted, except, did I?

How is it possible after twenty-two years to know so little about everything? I had said in the new therapist's office. No one had answered & you had said & I had said which was almost the same as saying ... almost but not quite. My voice always or never full of sleep is a way of saying "I want to be more in my body and less in my mind" or "less in my body and not so out-of-my-mind."

When you'd said to the therapist, I am not sure I can get what I want, I realized I had no idea what you wanted.

At least we don't disagree, you'd said, when I'd asked, as we'd left the new therapist's office, what you thought of him. Be-cause, I'd said, I thought he was *terrible*.

I'd said, I hope there's value in telling the same story over again to a new person, because it sure as hell costs a lot. I don't know why, but I was angry about the small hand towel neatly draped over the head of the leather couch that neither of us would ever lie down on.

To say it felt good in the almost dark, in the same bed, is not the same as saying it was what I wanted or what you wanted.

I was trying not to remember the Philosopher saying: *you just ... you were ... motherly ... a person who exuded a kind of ... you were someone I could say something like that to,* as he had said into my ear from whatever thank god faraway place he lives in. He'd said: *I thought it was a really cool dream ... I thought you'd want to know that according to my unconscious you'd done really well in life in the things that matter ...*

To say how I would afterward lie in bed listening to you sleeping, how I would ask you to leave by sitting up for a long time saying nothing, until you asked did I want you to leave, how I would say I don't care, which was a way of saying or a way of saying ...

To say how you gathered your pillows & wordlessly left the room & how I stayed up all night writing which is to say a way of leaving or staying full of you but not enough. More alone

than ever, not alone enough. Swimming, as I was, for so long
so far from shore. Longing to be anywhere but shorelined. My
motherly body a beatific disappointment. To say anything of
any of this is almost the same as saying "this long marriage"
which is almost the same as saying "what brings us here today
is" which is almost the same as saying nothing & too much.

# SEX WITH FAMOUS POET

I didn't tell you it happened because it didn't happen. Except early this morning in my dream when it *did*.

In real life (in class) last night a student said she liked "On Grace" by Danez Smith more than the selection of poems we read by Ronaldo Wilson from *Farther Traveler*.

"Liked" isn't the right word—, the student said.

This isn't *interesting*, a student interrupted, a student who didn't end up in my dream, but who, in real life, by which I mean class, said, This isn't *interesting*.

I later learned she felt that Ronaldo Wilson's "Double Life in Desire" was the *most* interesting poem she'd read all week but the way we were talking about it was boring or problematic or confusing or—

Everyone made a little sound when the student said, This isn't *interesting*.

I wasn't sure what was happening, was so tired, having not slept the night before, having confessed to not having slept to the students who knew full well & firsthand that this late-night teaching slot was nary no good for me.

Keep me on track, I said, No meandering! We need to read at least three poems, I said, And not as I am wont to do get lost in the woods of my own thinking. (In this case "woods" is a metaphor. All this takes place in NYC amidst the noise of the not-really-woods of my own thinking.)

Let's not forget, a student said, The *Q* stands for curious.
This confused me until fifteen minutes later I realized she'd said, The *Q* stands for questioning.

I'd been awake thirty-five hours, felt stoned-like, but wasn't, not yet. I was trying to remember who liked to be called queer, who definitely not & by which pronouns. I drew the schools of poetry as a planetary system on the whiteboard: the sun of lyric & twin moons of gender & sexual orientation created various eclipses as Confessional & New York School & Language & Beats orbited—

Excuse me, but what are you talking about? asked a student.

Hey, so, it's 7:30 p.m. and we've only read one poem and we did-n't even really talk about it, said a student.

I'm feeling super uncomfortable, said a student.

Are we talking about queer poets or queer poems or queer poets who are confessional? asked a student.

Just before class I'd asked the admin assist for "a yellow book of pop-ups" over & over despite his blank stare & finally took what I suddenly remembered were called Post-its off his desk, but I was so tired I couldn't remember what I'd wanted Post-its for.

Is a queer poem just a poem written by a queer poet? asked a student.

Yes, but not all queer poets write queer poems, said someone.

I'm feeling very uncomfortable, someone said, or maybe that's just what I was thinking.

Remember, I said, Last week, when seXpot said "a queer poem is a poem that disrupts the space"?

The students had been stony quiet when seXpot (her name's not seXpot obv) read her pornographic, non-normative, whore, cock, kink, queer, other-woman poems & later said they were not shocked not shocked *at all*. Well, *I* was shocked. I was thinking the only thing worse than admitting you have sex in a poem is admitting you don't. I was thinking admitting you have sex in a poem is not the same as admitting in a poem you have sex. I was thinking how I used to think "couple" meant "few" or "several" but after I got married the Husband always said, Couple means two. He'd been saying that for years, not in a romantic way, just for grammar's sake, but after we got married, he was "the Husband" so I had to say "after I got married the Husband always said," whereas before he was just a cis white guy mansplaining me. Anyway. After we got married, the Husband always said, Couple means two, whenever I said, for example, Hey bring me a couple of apples from the market (although I would have said "store" not "market"—poems can be so inaccurate). And over & over I'd be disappointed when he brought home exactly two. I want, you know, a whole bushel sometimes.

If I could only tell you (who even are you?) what it was like this morning to wake up knowing I was going to have to say to the Husband, I've got to tell you . . . you see . . . it just . . . happened . . . I had sex with [name of Famous Poet here] . . . Before confessing I wanted, at least, to remember if the sex was worth the dissolution of my shockingly long marriage. But the sex was so distant, like, like, like, like, like a word I couldn't recall for a familiar object. O middle-aged me, the sex was . . . it was . . . what's the word? . . . *dreamlike! Ai! Coup de foudre!* as I came to consciousness & realized I had nothing to confess. I had not slept with— & yet had I?

What is the word for the empty feeling of realizing something you believed happened didn't? But dreams happen. Don't they? I swear, I *saw* Famous Poet & me in a DC hotel room in my mind though he wasn't there & would swear it didn't happen & this would be true except I saw it & had feelings but who cares, there is no one waiting for me to bring him my dreams. What my dreams mean (if they mean anything) means nothing to anyone. But what is a poem if not a dream & is what happens here true?

What would you think, husband, reader, priest, if I told you how much I wanted to be writing this poem while I was frying salami (that's not a euphemism) for the salami egg & cheese on a bagel I was making my son the one who asked me Sunday if I was mentally ill, who said I was ruining his life because I want him to try out for basketball?

Maybe I am, I said, when he asked, Are you mentally ill? before walking away & slamming the door & if you must know I offered him fifty bucks—there I've said it fifty bucks—to suffer through looking like the no-shot-to-speak-of-soccer-player-trying-out-for-basketball whiteboy he is in front of the fast-breaking boys he wants to impress. Believe me, I know I'm ruining his life & was up all night feeling sorry for him & other feelings.

It's not a confessional poem unless it has shame, I said & drew a star on the board, the star of shame. This poem, for example, doesn't have enough shame yet to make it confessional. It's more NY School, don't you think? But where's my coterie? And it did feel pretty Bedlam on Sunday what with the screaming & cursing & teenage glaring. The Husband & I had just returned from three nights away during which we didn't have sex once but then after the fight with my son, Husband & I did. Then I was up all night, didn't sleep as they say a wink.

Do you think, asked a student, That the football in the Danez  Smith poem is a kind of drag?

There's nothing shocking about poems about pleasure or explicit sex or joy, said a student.

Really? I said, Even by women?

A student raised his/her/their eyebrows. I wondered if I was being terribly essentialist & remembered the semester I taught a class on the long poem & a queer Latinx student took off their—I think they were timberlands—& put on heels, stretching both feet out under the desk into the middle of the room. I knew it meant something but wasn't sure what.

Maybe I'm just old? I said, Or a prude? (No one said anything.)

I wasn't offended. I was too busy worrying whether I'd logged out upstairs. What if the g-chat between me & seXpot was still open in Anne Carson's office upstairs that I'm allowed to use when she's not there? I had texted seXpot right before class:

> **I'm starting to realize there's a day each month when I'm so cranky and angry nothing feels right and lately I think well what's bothering me I mean what in the fucking world do I want and it comes to me duh a good fucking but how could he know to fuck me if I'm so cranky angry anyway guess what? we did! even after you know who accused me of ruining his life and asked if I was mentally ill which duh almost killed the mood but didn't—we did it but then I couldn't sleep all fucking night just like the last time and the time**

**before that and spent all night awake knowing how fucked I was—how tired I'd be in class I can't tell if it's the sex or worrying about class or—**

**Hey!** seXpot interrupt-texted **For your birthday I'd like to get you a g-spot orgasm!**

**and how** I texted **do you propose to do that??**

seXpot sent a link to The Pleasure Chest UES "G Marks the Spot with Jes" & texted:

> **Buy whatever toy they recommend you know to help you "sleep."**

I was so tired I texted:

> **Great present thanks!** relieved she couldn't see my face.

Did I close the chat window or not? What if Anne Carson or some other famous poet was at that moment reading this exhausted ribaldry?

Bear with me, I said to the students & thought of entering "G Marks the Spot with Jes" Pleasure Chest Upper East Side workshop with a tame black bear on a leash shouting, Bear with me! Bear with me!

Ha HA! I said aloud. The students looked confused. I turned to the board & wrote:

**coterie v. direct address**

I said, What if a confessional poem is a poem written by a poet who has no friends, no coterie? A poem written to an unfriendly audience?

I wrote   **self-making**                **self-loathing**        on the whiteboard. I wrote                **dropping pearls**

I said, Quote, perverse sexuality interrupts the distinction between public and private space, close quote.

It was twenty hours since I'd had sex with the Husband & not slept all night. It was ten hours before I'd have sex with Famous Poet in my dream (this really happened, this class, this dream).

This isn't interesting, said a student who meant she wanted to talk about what we were talking about but not the way we were talking about it.

This is *not* shocking, said a student about Ronaldo Wilson's poem in which he describes watching pornography in which a woman has sex with older men in a theater while the woman's husband watches while filming.

Really? I said, Imagine going on the job market with these poems. Which is one of many stupid & beside the point things I said in class that night. I had enough trouble with my poems about having sex while pregnant, I said, Even though in my case I got pregnant from having sex, so why those poems shocked anyone is beyond me, but they did.

Someone rolled his/her/their eyes.
Teaching, I did not say, is 90% shame.
Maybe, I said, A confessional poem is a poem you think the poet can't survive.

My heart was beating like a just-caught fish slapping around on a splintery dock. I'd had two coffees after three weeks of no caffeine. Planet **BEATS** collided with **LANGUAGE** poetry. I wrote **performance** on the whiteboard. I wrote **SISSY** on the whiteboard. I wrote **MACHO**. I wrote **REALISM**.

The confessional poem says, I'm not who you think I am, I said. The confessional poem says I'm exactly who you think I am, I said.
This poem probably isn't queer, maybe questioning, I said.
The queer poem disrupts the space but doesn't want to be obvious to everyone, whereas the confessional poem wants to be obvious to absolutely everyone.
Yes, some queer poems are confessional yes some are not.

Maybe only white poets can write confessional poems, said Shane McCrae, when he visited class a few weeks back, Because white people feel they have fallen from grace whereas black people are considered to have already fallen from grace.

I wrote **RACE** on the whiteboard. I wrote

**METAPHOR MYTH CODE RISK**

I suspect the editor will suggest I take the names out of this poem & whether naming is an act of recognition & intimacy or violence & objectification [**all sex is about power** texted seXpot just as I silenced my phone] is what this poem, I mean class, I mean poem, I mean essay, is about. I wrote **LIVED EXPERIENCE** on the whiteboard.

Why does Sharon Olds get called Confessional but not Lucille Clifton?
What gives you permission? I asked the students, Or are you writing a poetry of opposition?

A few weeks earlier, after reading my most confessional poems in a part of America famous for the killing of a black man by the police, which is to say *in America*, a black student thanked me for writing about race & I felt ashamed of how much I desired his approval for having performed the role of "good white person."

The confessional poem runs after that shame, runs after the shame of running after his approval, I said to the students without explaining who "he" is.

(Later I will go home in a taxi that costs $17.95 & get high & not have sex but will still wake up in the middle of the night to write this poem. I will drag myself to the fancy school where first graders will ask me why I'm a poet & I will say, Poetry lets me make invisible bridges between me and the reader. And the blondest boy I've ever seen will say, And it's good when those bridges break because then you know you're all alone & I will stare at the boy & later stand outside Everyman Espresso on Thirteenth & Third & read this poem to D A Powell & tell him about the blond boy & the bridges & Doug will say, But you're not actually going to use his name right (meaning the name of Famous Poet not the blond boy) & months later I'll read this poem in Austin, TX & a poetry professor will come up after-wards & say, That's very brave the way you name him & I will say, I have no idea what you're talking about, I don't even know him, I just like his poems and dreamed about having sex with him & later I *will* know what she is talking about & I will wonder whether he did what they said he did & if he did, are the women OK & whether this means I really shouldn't after all or should after all use his name.)

Great class, said a student, when we were out on the steps & he was dragging on a cigarette & I was resisting the urge to say Smoking kills. We were watching mice run around in the night, some of them making their way back to our classroom, where I know they live. I was stalling. Not wanting to ride home on the brightly lit subway where anyone could see me covered in the shame of teaching, of writing, of wanting poems more than my children, of wanting to go home & get high & finally sleep more than have sex. Turns out this is a confessional poem in which I confess to sex that never happened, awash in the shame I rightly deserve.

## THE FEELING

She didn't have a name for it but had felt it before.

She could only breathe if she thought of herself in third person. So she thought of herself in third person whenever possible. For example: "She and the Husband had been fucking with unusual frequency as if in training for something, but last night it took them a long time to get off."

That "long time" was part of the feeling she'd felt before but couldn't name. She wondered whether thinking of herself as "she" was making it difficult to be in her body.

## ENOUGH IS ENOUGH

She wanted to feel to keep feeling her naked body against the scratchy blanket she'd gotten, not *from* her mother, but along with everything her mother had left behind, which was everything her mother had owned.

It felt good to feel to keep feeling the scratchy wool against her skin instead of climbing in between the cool, smooth sheets. She wanted to keep feeling her skin against the rough blanket after being fucked, after *she* had fucked the Husband who'd earlier texted **I have a proposal for you if you get home in the next 30 minutes**.

She had turned to Olena & said, Look at this text—it's because we've got couples therapy tomorrow, she'd said & she told Olena she really should go home. She told Olena she never went anywhere on weeknights or did anything, ever. Really? Olena had said. (This was when they were out with whiteguy, drinking rye whiskey & talking about memoir.)

You're a white dude, Olena had said to whiteguy, when white-guy had said, It just matters if it's good, not who wrote it, when whiteguy had said, *I decide* that's who, when she had said, But part of what you mean by "good" has to do with who wrote it and who you are. And who decides what's good is partly based on who you are, she said, after whiteguy had said, Who cares who wrote something? Who cares if the writer is black or white, female or male, gay or whatever? Why can't you just read what's good? when she'd told him about the class she was teaching that Olena had visited earlier that evening. (This was when they were drinking rye whiskey & talking about memoir & telling whiteguy about the class she was teaching that Olena had visited earlier that evening.)

Well, maybe *memoir*, whiteguy said, when she'd said, It was prose, when whiteguy had said, Poems can't kill people, when she'd said, Or I killed her, when whiteguy had said, So she died on purpose? after she'd told him the story of her mother's death & the book she'd written that her mother hadn't wanted her to publish, when Olena'd said, You're fine, you're fine, it's all fine, when she'd said, But I've lost friends, maybe jobs, when Olena'd said, You've got to just write your shit, when she'd said, No one likes to be objectified, when Olena'd said, Really? That bothers people? when she'd said, Oh Olena I was scared shitless you'd be angry because I wrote about you and we barely know each other and I was scared you'd recognize yourself in my poems even though I didn't use your name (although she had used Olena's name), when Olena'd said, In this life I'd never be angry with you for that, when she'd said, Oh shit, when Olena'd said, out of the blue, By the way I *do* pick up my kids on time from school, which was obviously a response to a poem she'd written about Olena, even though she knew nothing at all about Olena, except what she knew about Olena from Olena's poems.

(This was when they were drinking rye whiskey & talking about the ethical considerations of representing real people in art & about her memoir *MOTHERs* in which she'd written "I go to see the poet Olena Kalytiak Davis read at NYU. She is drunk. She is late for her own reading. She is drunk, and she is amazing. She scares me. She is thin and sexy and dirty. Her pants are ripped, 80s style, and she strokes the exposed skin of her thighs as she reads. She scares me. I envy. She feels real to my faux. Her infidelity to my New York. Her Alaska to my monogamy. My sober. My timeliness. My jobfulness. My marriage. My flabby belly no matter how often or far I run. My Jewish. My living mother. My other. My baby. My husband, same age, only sometimes my lover. My —what does Alice Notley think of her? I'm blind with jealousy for a moment as if Olena were my sister and Alice our mother. And if she were, what would Mother Alice say? Why can't you be more like your crazy drunk sister Olena? Maybe Alice would. Maybe she would" & her book *The Pedestrians* in which she'd written "Last night the Post-Confessional Poet said, 'I don't know how many poets stand up at a reading and tell you how bad they're doing—I'm doing real bad.' Later she said, 'Now we put toothbrushes up assholes in poems all the time,'" & "Who picks her kids up on time? I wondered," in which the Post-Confessional Poet was Olena.)

I like one ice cube too, said whiteguy, when she'd said, One ice cube. I like rye, you like rye, said whiteguy, when she'd pointed & asked, Well what's that bottle on the top shelf? & the waiter had gone to check & had come back & said, Rye, after she'd asked if they had rye & the waiter had said, We don't have rye. (This was when they'd just sat down at the Singaporean restaurant that whiteguy had suggested they go to for dinner & a drink.)

Wouldn't you like to know, she said, when Olena'd said, I love it & whiteguy had said, Famous poet? when she'd told them, for example, she'd recently written a poem called "Sex with Famous Poet" & said, But what did he ever do to me, nothing. (This was when they were waiting for a table at the Singaporean restaurant.)

You're fine, Olena said, when she'd told Olena maybe she had a fetish a compulsion to write unpublishable poems then publish them, write unreadable poems then read them & maybe this was partly because she was such a good glrl in real life. Maybe she felt she had the right to be bad in poems. (This was when they were waiting for a table at the Singaporean restaurant.)

It would blow your mind, Olena said, when she'd said, Come on tell us married people if it's really all that, when Olena was talking about sex with someone new, Olena wouldn't say who, after she'd said she hadn't had sex with anyone except her husband since 1993 & whiteguy had said he'd been married twenty years, which was not, she realized, the same as saying he hadn't had sex with other women for twenty years, when she'd said, Well my husband knows I'm into graying hair, nodding at whiteguy, when Olena'd said, What would your husband think about him being here? nodding at whiteguy with his graying hair, when she'd said, My husband is a little afraid of you, the you being Olena (This was when they were on their way to the Singaporean restaurant whiteguy had picked.)

He broke all the rules, she said, Everything was cropped weird and grainy he was going for emotional truth instead of technical virtuosity, lots of people thought it was shit, but the book changed everything, she'd said when Olena'd said, No & white-guy had said, Sure, when she'd asked, Do you know the photographer Robert Frank? when Olena'd, said Really? when she'd said, Well I wanted to know how bad I could make the poems and still make a good book, when Olena'd said, I didn't care much for each poem but I loved your last book, when she'd said, Thanks, when Olena'd said, I like that your city has a "my" and your husband has a "the," as they were walking to the restaurant that served Singaporean food that whiteguy had picked.

I'm not hungry, she said after the graying-haired whiteguy had said, Come on & Olena'd said, Come on & she'd said, I'm afraid of you, to Olena & whiteguy had said, Nothing will happen to you & the student she'd been talking to said, Well that's creepy, or maybe she'd said, That's creepy, when Olena & some white guy had come back to ask if she was hungry while she was talking to a very tall student outside the classroom. The student had just said, I understand Olena's work better now after hearing her speak & she'd said, Isn't that another kind of reading biography into a poem—being able to understand someone's work after hearing them speak or meeting them in person? (This was just after Olena had visited her class called The Legacy of the Confessional Impulse.)

Maybe we can apply these ethical questions to other genres? Maybe it will be easier when we're not talking about poetry? she'd said, when she'd reminded them that next week they'd be talking about standup comedy & artist books & performance artists & the movie *Stories We Tell* & asked, Is anyone willing to talk about rap and hip-hop? when a student had said, We were supposed to talk about the difference between Utilitarian and Kantian notions of ethics and the potential exploitation of writing about others but we're way off the outline you gave us, when she'd just sat there after Olena'd left, when she'd said, It might take me a while to recover from that, when she'd said, Well that was a mind fuck, when a student had asked, Can we do a show of hands: who felt that was productive? when the students had said, We all wrote that down, when she'd said, I've got the title for my next book: "Boringest Fuckshow on the Planet Earth," which was something Olena had just said in class.

The only thing I'm sure of is doubt, she said, when a student had said, Yes! Olena does that all the time in her poems and I don't understand it when someone says something and then says the opposite like when Olena said "I didn't learn dick but I learned everything," when a student had said, When the guy in *The Breakfast Club* says he has a gun but it's a flare gun that doesn't mean the feelings aren't real, when she'd said, One of

the criticisms of Olena's work and my work is that we are priv-
ileged white women and are not really in danger, when a stu-
dent had said, I found it very reassuring the way Olena talked
about counteracting anxiety with ecstasy, when another stu-
dent had said, I want to go to sleep for a month I was so worried
about Olena, when she'd said, I'm thinking about Robert Capa's
D-Day photos that are blurry, overexposed, overdeveloped, and
the way the technical flaws are markers of the fact that he was
in real danger and if I found out he'd messed the photos up on
purpose I'd be pretty pissed off and I do feel Olena's in danger
maybe that's what makes the work confessional, when a stu-
dent had said, I want to comfort her, after Olena had talked al-
most nonstop for fifty minutes saying things like "for example
yes of course and at the same time no!" when a student had
asked, Is there an "I" outside of race gender and class?

What Rachel's trying to say, a student said, Is do you think being
a good person in real life makes you want to break the rules in
poems? when Olena'd said, I don't understand what you're ask-
ing, is that even a question? when she'd said, Do you think that
makes you want to break the rules or hurt people in your
poems? when Olena'd said, I'm a very good person, after return-
ing from her quick drink with Major Jackson & said, Neo-con-
fessional? You made that up didn't you?

A pushover, she said, when a student had asked, What's that? when she'd said, I'm a patsy, when Olena'd come in at 7:05 p.m. & said, I know we said 7 p.m. but can I go for a quick drink with Major? & had gone for a quick drink with Major after she'd said, OK but slam it down.

What if writing is not about language, but about loneliness? she said, What if you don't believe you exist? she'd said, when no one had said anything, when she'd asked, Can anyone speak to that? Can anyone think of why someone would like that or would want that? when a student had said I wouldn't want anyone to read my biography into my work, why would anyone want that?

Can we just say "What's your relationship with Robert Lowell"? she asked when she couldn't understand the question a student had wanted her to ask Olena who was about to visit their class.

**WHO ARE YOU WRITING FOR?** she'd written on the board.
**IS THERE SOMETHING OR SOMEONE YOU WON'T WRITE ABOUT?** she'd written on the board.
**IS THERE ONE "I" OR ARE THERE MULTIPLE "I"S?**
**IS THERE AN "I" OUTSIDE RACE GENDER AND CLASS?**

**DO YOU BELIEVE IN TRUTH?**

**DEFINE CONFESSIONAL.**

**ARE YOU CONFESSIONAL?**

**HOW DO YOU FEEL ABOUT BEING CALLED CONFESSIONAL OR POST-CONFESSIONAL OR NEO-CONFESSIONAL?** she'd written on the board, when a student had said, Your outline says we should be preparing for Olena's visit, when she'd said, Maybe if you assume your readers are all post-confessional or post-truth in the sense that there is no truth and no need for confession in the age of reality TV and Facebook and Instagram, then you can write anything and maybe you have no ethical problems as a writer because no one has the expectation that what you write is true even if you told them over and over it was true and the work is powered by the engine of exposure and risk of truth telling.

So, it's all just moral relativity? she said, when a student had said, We each need to decide for ourselves what's right when we're talking about a kind of poetry that breaks personal con-fidences and reveals something someone doesn't want re-vealed and the poem or poet profits from this exposure, when she'd asked, Well, who gets to decide? And if it's for the greater good, as you say, if the ends justify the means, as you say, is that based on content and if so what kind of content? Abuse trauma racism? Or is "the ends justify the means" a matter of how good the poem turns out to be? when she'd pointed to the whiteboard where she'd written & circled the word **WORLD** & written & circled the word **SELF** & drawn a dotted line between them.

Isn't that what we want a poem to do? she said, Not the violence part but the re-enact part? Don't we want poems to not just recall experience but be an experience, although, yes, we did say maybe the original Confessional poets re-traumatized themselves with their poems rather than used poems to integrate their experiences and that's part of what makes us voyeurs, part of the charge we pay for the eyeing of Plath's scars, when a student had asked, But what about what Roger Reeves said about not wanting the poem to re-enact violence? when she'd said, For some readers there's no amount of self they won't devour, some people want a person naked and more naked and more naked in a room of mirrors, some people like that, she'd said & had written **SELF** on the board.

But is there a titration point, she asked when a student had said, Actually, I felt annoyed when Olena included words in Serb or Slovakian with no translation but even when Olena writes in English I feel like I'm forced to read from behind a mirror in which Olena checks herself out, when she'd asked, What if the poet avoids implicating herself and tries to write all and only about **THE WORLD** and what if the poet writes all and only about **THE SELF**?

Let's get to work, she said, Let's not forget our outline, she'd said, Let's stay on track today, she'd said, after hustling to office hours after lunch with her favorite San Fran poet who'd said, Oh I guess you have to, when he saw she had to because the little package was sealed, when San Fran had said, Oh don't rip it just smell it, when they were standing on Eighty-First Street & San Fran had given her the lovely present after taking her out to lunch during which she'd told San Fran that Olena Davis was visiting class later & had said, I don't know why Olena's work is so important to me, she'd said, It might say something bad about me, which is not to say anything bad about Olena's work, which is not to say I wouldn't say something bad about Olena's work if I had something bad to say since lately I seem compelled to say bad things aloud or in poems, although I'm not even sure that what I'm writing are poems, they might just be words that say bad things or bad things made of words.

Hey, why don't you just read that new poem? San Fran asked when she'd bemoaned the sorry state of her unfinished lectures

& told San Fran that in an online article about Olena there was a sidebar of links titled "A Brief History of 'Confessional' Poems" which included a link to a poem by San Fran that neither San Fran nor she considered the least bit confessional which didn't mean much since she'd lost sight of what made a poem confessional even though she was teaching a whole class about that & writing a lecture about it & even after all this time & all this talking & thinking she wondered if liking Olena was like liking her own reflection even though looking at Olena was not like looking in a mirror, it was like watching Britta Phillips sing "Listen, the Snow is Falling" on stage, Britta's heavy, red electric bass strapped to her willow-thin frame, which is to say the feeling of looking at Olena was the continuous present of looking at the most beautiful woman in the world which she was not & never would be & not at all like looking at her own reflection & the feeling of knowing she could never go back in time even though the past was always with her & she wanted to feel to keep feeling the coarse wool against her bare skin until she couldn't stand that feeling anymore.

# AND STILL I SPEAK OF IT

**What a beautiful day** Dan texts.

**I know nothing about it** I respond.

My radio in the kitchen keeps itself company inside the muted drilling from outside my window.

*The United States cares about mankind* says the Brigadier General in my kitchen.

> *... it would have to include hostage negotiation*

> *... those taking part are called belligerents*

> *... get the girls back get them back get them back*

Yesterday a girl jumped from her grandmother's roof one block from here. The doorman found her. The girl's parents papered the building with letters asking no one to speak of it.

# IT HAS COME TO MY ATTENTION

His work has been translated into fourteen languages, Soren said, introducing a fiction writer at the undergrad faculty reading.

"His work has been translated into fourteen languages and no one understands it," she wrote in her notebook.

It was the first thing she'd written, not nice, of course (not even true in this case) for many months other than to-dos or grocery lists, doctors' phone numbers & the names of her new students with identifying details such as preferred pronouns, pronunciation mnemonics, which colleges they'd dropped out of/transferred from & who was living at home/who in NY for his/her/their first time.

Favorite poets? Sylvia Plath, Louise Glück, T. S. Eliot, Sylvia Plath, Sylvia Plath & seriously—Shel Silverstein? Favorite culture makers? Jill Soloway, J. K. Rowling, Billy Joel & seriously—Nietzsche?

She didn't write "Nietzsche" in her notebook but kept remembering that one of them had said Nietzsche & realized, after months of no writing other than to-dos, grocery lists & doctors' phone numbers that writing might be a way of remembering but not writing didn't mean she would/could/should forget.

She wrote: "I feel as free as a squirrel" in her notebook which was a line from she/her/hers born in China, just-back-from-medical-leave, rising-sophomore's poem.

The meds won't make you not you, the MD said. The boy looked everywhere in the room.

"The baby was so little I began to have enemies," wrote living poet Sarah Vap in an as-of-yet unpublished manuscript. She wanted to tell Sarah everything. But the privacy agreement now folded & balanced on the boy's knee that she & the boy had just signed—what about that? The boy was a few weeks shy of 18. Could she? Would she? Should she tell Sarah or anyone everything/anything?

She was trying to answer the questions when they were her questions to answer. She was trying to let some of the molecules in the room go unnoticed so she could answer the questions that were her questions to answer. She could not pay attention to everything always, could she? Could she pay attention now but *not* write it later? Pay attention now, but later *not* remember? Could she be a sieve catching the larger stones & let the smaller ones flow back into the muddy river, then, turn the whole self over, letting everything/anything—the words, the boy, the world—go? Every small or large, rough & not yet cut, was potentially precious. Who was she to judge?

"I can feel myself going away," she meant to write. She did not write.

She sat in the room that was at that moment an office, at that moment painful. Later a bedroom, a living room, many kinds of rooms & all these rooms newsrooms>>>  <<<waves & satellites seeping, reaching—

The only student in the classroom whose pronouns were he/him/his used the word "moment" five times in fifteen lines, which seemed fine to her, not a flaw at all, but he/him/his was concerned: his sonnet was fifteen lines. He wanted to know which line to cut, which idea, what image?

The person talking, she thought, Is sometimes me. Often "I" is the person crying. Could she be less susceptible? Less *in relation* to everything/everyone?

"Drones are probably killing someone right now," Sarah Vap's poem reminded at the top & bottom of every page for hundreds of pages. Could she afford to pay attention/stop paying attention?

"Same-same," she sometimes said when she agreed with someone. "Same," she said when anyone asked, "How are you?" & everything was still so [      ]. This is just how I feel right now, was a mantra she'd used during childbirth & many other moments since.

"This is just how I feel right now."

Moment, moment, moment, moment, moment. Moment, moment, moment, moment, moment. This is just how I feel right now.

I can feel myself going away, she meant to write. She did not. Nor did she. I mean: go away. I mean: write.

What dead poet Bob Creeley was saying when he wrote, "Love, if you love me, / lie next to me" she tried to explain to the students. The effect of the word "despond" in dead poet Gwendolyn Brooks's line "and other symptoms of an old despond." She tried to explain to the students: diction, meter, narrative, image.

Writing as a way of paying attention. But something had happened in Manchester. She was trying so hard not to see, hear, feel. It was the latest something that had happened *in*, something that had happened *to*, something that had happened that she could not bear to see/not see, hear/not hear. How can anyone hold all this rough let alone the muddy river?

Every metaphor is full of blood diamonds, full of blood. The act of making one thing into other. Trees into pulp into paper. People into image, sound, word, story.

Some of the parents were there to pick up their teenagers who are now orphans, someone said.

Her eyes were tired of seeing but she was driving or walking or awake or alive. There was no way to close her eyes. She could turn off the radio but could not stop hearing, reading, being porous. Sarah Vap had described writing or was it living as "extreme susceptibility" & what anyway would it mean to turn away? To *stop* paying attention? To stop writing, stop making anything into anything, to forgo the "tearful tale of bale and barge" that Brooks described, the "tiredness, the fatuousness, the semi- / lust of intentional indifference" that Creeley despised?

Would there then be actual bodies? Would the blood by which I mean violence on her white hands be the color of blood by which I mean the red liquid that circulates in the arteries & veins of human & other vertebrate animals? Would the people her people had killed, by inaction or subtle or overt action, rise up embodied to lie with *her people* by which I mean of common descent or lineage? Her, as we say, *blood* by which I mean kin who had been killed by the inaction or subtle or overt actions of people who were not *her people* as defined by bloodlines or *as if* bloodlines or *as if* killing *as if* actual *as if* rising up *as if* lie *as if* she were *of* a people any more than of any *other* people full of blood out for blood bad blood flesh & blood blood money blood boiling in cold blood blood relation relative.

She tried to tell the boy she felt this way, had felt this way, *feels*? She tried not to tell him.

*У*

They're not happy pills, the MD says.
Make that a double, she joke-thought.


Remember, a friend says, That Joseph Campbell thing about a
hero is someone who transitions from dependence to inde-
pendence?


It's a big fucking deal, a friend says, What he's going through.
Don't be a hero, someone says.
Hero is as hero does, she thinks.
She thinks: here oh, here oh, here.


Moment, moment, moment. Fourteen languages. Fifteen lines.


Would you feel this way if he had a broken leg? a friend asks.
Diabetes? a friend asks.
This is terribly common, a friend says.


Put on your oxygen mask before assisting your child or other
passengers, they caution as she prepares to leave the literal
ground or when she says, writes, texts, emails: "I cannot keep
on [      ]"

Take care, someone says.

Take care of *yourself*, someone says.

Fuck you, she thinks.

What summer plans? she thinks.

She crosses out words in a student's poem until the last line reads "the mirror is empty. I drown in it." Why not, she thinks, if they all love Plath so, so much? Still, who was she to cut anyone's lines?

Is the rhyme OK? a student asks.

Do you get what I mean? a student asks.

Syntax, form, musicality of language. Repetition, punctuation, lineation, alliteration. A mother should not be in the room to hear her son, no matter what age, answer these diagnostic questions.

The boy looks everywhere in the room. The MD looks too carefully at the boy, except when writing longhand on lined paper during which she & the boy watch the MD writing longhand on a blue-lined, white pad that they are just far enough away not to be able to read. She wonders if the boy is also remembering that on the folded agreement now resting on the boy's jeaned knee it is written: "You do not have the right to request the therapist's notes."

Are the therapist's notes a way of remembering or forgetting? she wonders. She wonders whether the MD's methodical writing is a way to draw the boy in words on the page or an excuse to look away so the boy can stop looking everywhere else in the room & for a moment safely take in the white-haired MD, head slightly bowed, hand moving left to right across the blue-lined, white pages. A precious near-silence as he writes. A way of resting in the present before the next question, series of questions, that attempt to, through language, assess the boy's physical & mental experience, the boy's personal & family history. A series of questions to distill the boy's past & present temperamental situational developmental historical political individual internal physiological cultural geographical biological predispositional post-lapsarian epigenetic genetic familial societal specific particulars into a diagnosis that would be rendered into pills the same size (but not weight) as the tiny diamonds that kept the boy's ancestors alive long enough to make those who would make those who would make this boy, some of which & some of whom may have been some of what makes the boy feel or not feel, be or not be, in need of pills slightly smaller in diameter than a one-carat diamond.

In this silence they can look at the MD & she can think of all the questions he is not asking the boy, the answers to which might better explain how the boy had come to be who he was & how the boy has more recently come to be, as they refer to it, "not himself."

Such as: how many homeless people do you stop to speak with on a typical day? How did you know Donald Trump would win the presidency? How many documentaries have you seen? How many books by Paul Auster, Philip Roth, Herman Melville, Claudia Rankine, James Baldwin & Ram Dass have you read? How many plays by William Shakespeare? How many stories by Rabbi Nachman of Bratslav? How many hours a day do you listen to left-leaning political podcasts or standup by mentally ill or substance-abusing comedians? How many times a day do you read the comments on Breitbart? How many articles in the *New York Times*, *Washington Post*, *Haaretz*, *The Atlantic*, *Slate*, *The New Republic*? Are you straight, white, cis, male-identified, able-bodied, economically geographically educationally privileged & fourteen days shy of being a legal adult? What exactly have you done today to dismantle white supremacy, the heteropatriarchy & toxic masculinity? How did you feel when you stopped chanting outside Chuck Schumer's home each Tuesday with that bunch of hippies?

What upsets you most: the murders of Harvey Milk Malcolm X MLK jr Eric Garner, the economic oppression of 90% of the world's population, the prison-industrial complex, systematic government-sanctioned worldwide violence against women, the current global refugee crisis, the devastation & destruction of the environment, or the decimation of native populations? How many voters were you personally able to register in Pennsylvania? How effective were your hours of phone banking? What made you feel you had to leave math class? Why were you unable to perform in the jazz show?

She tried, later, to explain all this to the Husband, who was also Father to the boy, the same boy they had seen, who had once *been*, a moving, black-&-white form on a monitor in an exam room. A moving, humanlike form sharing the space called womb with a still form, an unforming form—too still—the form's humanlike face turned away, the unborn him/her/them twin who would not come to be but *was* even when language could not make sense of it or make it/him/her/them make sense. They believed these images to be *the representation of* or *a window unto* the inside of her body. Here's your baby, said the technician, pressing a gel-covered plastic tool called a wand into her side, the fetal heart a blinking star or so they claimed.

More than 18 years ago she had written/tried to write (so many years ago) how there was something uncanny, nearly traumatic, about seeing the inside of one's body. Seeing, inside one's body, an unborn form of baby next to an unforming baby but not just because "vanishing twin," as the diagnosis goes. And now the live one, the "singleton" as they called the one who would become this boy, in the room with the MD asking—

It has come to my attention, she says to the students who are young eager broken or breaking.

It has come to my attention, she says, after the introductions, after the creative nonfiction writer, the fiction writer, the poet & the other creative nonfiction writer who read from a novel-in-progress about a writer with his very own same name.

It has come to my attention, she says. She is the last reader, because of alphabetical order, at the faculty reading for the Writers in New York summer program in the downstairs parlor of the converted brownstone. It is one hour after class, three hours after her lunch with the boy at Niu Noodles where she'd ordered duck lettuce-wraps & he'd gotten fried rice & she couldn't taste anything but liked the combination of textures & the boy joke-asked, Why are all your kids so fucked up?

The boy asked if she felt responsible or guilty for her fucked-up kids even though the boy said he didn't think this was really her fault. She had an urgent desire to record the boy, his words, these words which pierced her motherheart.

All she wanted was to record *everything*: her guilt, his speaking, his breathing that had once been her breath. To draw, even though she did not know how, the curve of his shoulders, to see hear know measure hold report the blinking star of his heart. All she wanted was to move closer to him, to hold him & hold him but he had never much liked being held & doing so was less & less possible. More & more words were the only way to touch him in this room which was the room of moving away, the room of knowing she could not hold him.

She had never felt so similar to anyone, not even herself, as when she looked at the boy. It was a mirror it was empty she was drowning.

The second creative nonfiction writer grimaces when she says, during the faculty reading, Terrible place. When she says, It has come to my attention that the world is a terrible place.

Many of you came here to become better writers, which is an admirable goal, but maybe it's not about becoming a better writer, she says.

How can she explain, when the most important parts of her are invisible? Did it matter to them to anyone that she had a uterus & had used it such that so that & from the waters had brought forth? What would she be without the boy, the boys?

What Creeley meant, she tries to explain to the students. For fuck's sake, something/someone come close, come *through* the same, same, same, the I, I, I, of the rain, persistent, insistent aliveness, the doubt, the on & on & ongoingness.

See the alliteration—"tearful tale" & "bale and barge"?—in Brooks's poem?

The rhymes—"tale" & "bale," "large" & "barge," "despond" & "bond"? Remember, she says to the students, We say "rhymes *with*" not "rhymes *to*." She has no idea what she's getting at.

What's the effect, she asks, Of Brooks choosing "despond" instead of "sadness"? No one answers.

While they write in their notebooks she plays Paul Robeson & tries to decide what to say & read at the faculty reading. While the students write, the boy is at home, sleeping instead of finishing a paper on the drug trade in South America, instead of completing his reading reflection on *The Lives of Animals* by Coetzee. Sleeping instead of proving something with calculus or logging his service hours at the men's homeless shelter. Paul Robeson sings "Go Down Moses" & the boy sleeps & the students write & she sits, listening, trying not to listen. Waiting, wondering, knowing Nazis are rising up everywhere & there is shoving on the subway, shootings on the street, the police murdering hurting harming people we currently call people of color & other othered others everywhere. Human forms turned away from each other: bordered, detained, toxic poisons seeping creeping across the borderless natural world.

Hatred, fear, panic, the press of history. The moment moment moment rain of it, on & on, our preferential babies a constant patter, a pattern.

Creeley is saying, she tries to explain to the students.
Creeley is saying *come through this sameness.*
Someone/something *come close* enough to touch, to *touch me.*

Have you ever? Do you? Have you had thoughts of? asks the MD. The boy looks everywhere in the room. This is the only thing we have not fully discussed, says the boy, nodding at her, not looking at her.

It's interesting, a friend says, Your use of third person. Have you ever tried second?
I'm afraid to use "you," she says not knowing what she means, knowing this is a diagnostic question.

"We are each other's harvest," wrote Gwendolyn Brooks.
"We are each other's business," wrote Brooks.
"We are each other's magnitude and bond."

She looks at her boy who is her business, is her harvest, is her magnitude & right now, a tearful tale.

Who would "you" even be? She? He? We?

In their domestic spaces & moments, walks & dinners, lunches & living rooms, the boy says, This is how fascism takes hold. The boy says, The world is a bad place.

When she goes into his room to ask why he just hurled his iPad to the ground the boy says, Thirty percent of the world's population is suffering beyond comprehension and what is anyone doing about it?

He is not wrong. He is reading Camus. He is not going out. He is sleeping again. He knows all the genocides. He is doing a KenKen, putting numbers in boxes based on complicated calculations. He understands numbers & what they mean. Not these numbers. The other numbers. The numbers that mean people. He knows all the names for Nazis.

He is too smart for his own good, someone says.
It's good he's going through this now instead of later, someone says.

He is sleeping. He is napping. He never naps. He is napping.

It has come to my attention, she tells the assembled students, That the world is a terrible place. The faces of the faculty change.

I know this from watching the news, she says. I know this from my sons. The students are so young. They are looking at her. Some are just a year or so older than the boy.

The boy's father texts, **I will try to come home happy at 6:20.**
He who was Husband is mostly Father. She is Mother only.
Woman never. Writer underwater.

She is crying in her office, which is not her office. She has fifteen
minutes before class. Thirteen minutes. I am going to be late
because I am having a panic attack sorry, the pink-haired stu-
dent emails her eleven minutes before class. She prints "Paul
Robeson" by Gwendolyn Brooks. She prints "The Rain" by Rob-
ert Creeley. She prints her long poem she will probably read,
probably shouldn't read, at the faculty reading.

Tell me more about sadness, says the MD to the boy who is look-
ing everywhere else in the room. I'm against it, says the boy.

But the MD is humorless. The MD is a pillar of diagnostic inte-
grity. The MD does not know the boy from Adam or the woman
from Adam's mother. And who anyway was Adam's mother?
Birdsong? Ocean? Pure oxygen?

*Who* will come close? She wants Creeley to answer her.

Love, if you love me, who are you? *Tell me.*

*My boy*, you say, you think, you write. "You" cannot write like this. The "you" must be the boy. The boy must be. He must be brought close though he seems unwilling, unable, unavailable. You must *make* him—what?—you cannot make him. You made him, but not of, not with, words.

No mother should watch a man in a tie ask her son these questions. No mother should let a man in a tie ask her son these questions no matter what age no matter what room without her there.

So many of my friends are blowing up their lives, a friend says, With affairs, quitting jobs, divorces. I'm throwing my body over my life but it's blowing up anyway, she tells her friend.

Her preferred pronouns were I, me, mine but living poet Brian Teare said, Maybe don't put "I" at the center of all poems all the time. Anyway, "I" wasn't a pronoun anyone would call her & maybe she needed to stand back & see herself to feel herself going away. How else could "I" stay, stand to stay? No one was calling her except everyone was calling her, such as, via email: "I am having a panic attack." Such as the text **I will try to come**

**home happy at 6:20**. Such as the question "how long have you been sleeping in separate rooms?" Such as the answer to that question. Such as "while we did really enjoy our conversation with you and very much admire your work, we ended up making an offer to someone else, and that person has accepted the offer." Such as "how many nights will you be away from your children?" Such as "it might not be a good time to be away." Such as "the side effects kick in before the benefits which is why we start with a low dose." Such as "there is some research that in adolescents . . ." Such as "an increased desire for carbohydrates." Such as "what are you writing?" Such as "are you writing?" Such as: the MD's questions, the MD's description diagnosis verdict detection summary such as: the side effects of versus the side effects of—

Have you ever thought of—
Have you ever thought of—

Have you ever thought of—
Have you ever thought of—?

How do I put myself more in the poem? a student asks.
Describe the world, she answers.
Is it clear that the poem is about my mom? a student asks.

I like the line, the students say to each other.
Maybe try . . . they say.
What about . . .? they say to each other.

What if you just took out . . . ?

The heart, the engine, risk, meter, image, meaning of the poem.

The poem would be better if . . . Better if, better if you, if you just, just tried.

Now that my kids are people I can't write about them, a poet mom said.
I can feel myself going away, she means to write.
I can feel myself going away, is all she can imagine writing if she could imagine writing.

I can feel myself going away, is all she can write if she doesn't write about the boy.
I can feel myself going away, I writes.

Maybe learning to write is about finding a way to *live better*, she says, into the mic, when it's finally her turn, before she reads the long poem about her sons who are people now, people she shouldn't be writing about, after she says, It has come to my attention that the world is a terrible place. After reading "The Rain" by Robert Creeley & "Paul Robeson" by Gwendolyn Brooks & spending six & a half minutes on each of the students' poems: moment, moment, moment, moment, moment, moment, mo—how might she/he/they revise toward strangeness intimacy greater density of language?

She used to say, Where's the risk?
She used to say, *Always* be specific. Be *more specific*.
You can't be too specific, she used to say.
Let me see it, feel it, care about it, she once advised.

But now, she didn't want them to risk anything. Each of them was someone's son/daughter/child. She didn't want to know what was at stake, didn't want to say which lines to cut, didn't want to correct anyone's English. Maybe the street *was* "scattered of people" as she/her/hers had written. Maybe "I feel free as a squirrel" was exactly the right simile. "Tablet" is something people used to write on, but now mostly refers to something we swallow. What if this is, this writing is, the only way for her to—?

I tries *not* to correct, *not* to remember, *not* to write, *not* to pay attention, but I sees hears remembers writes. I tries to tell the boy, Until this moment I had not realized that one of my fundamental beliefs from the time I was your age, maybe younger, was that there is value in describing my experience/feelings to others and that belief is the basis of my life's work and my understanding of art. I don't know why I imagined there was an audience wanting caring needing to know who I am, what I think/feel, but once I imagined it, I needed to believe.

This audience, without which, I don't know how I—she can't finish the sentence.

Her pronouns are I, my, mine, mother, which is to say *one with another.*

She was the speaker weeping in the office that is not hers after minced duck in lettuce cups with the boy who said, I don't believe in God and I don't believe in a soul, so how can the medicine *not* change who I am if my body is what I am? She was suffering what Sarah Vap called extreme susceptibility the onset of which was sudden & gradual.

Are you mostly Ashkenazi? a well-meaning teacher asked the boy. Have you read *The Communist Manifesto*? Clarice Lispector? Have you tried meditation, exercise, gardening?
The prom is a very non-prom, a well-meaning administrator told the boy.

Get a notebook you wouldn't usually use, living poet Erika Meitner had advised her, And a pen you wouldn't usually use, and write a poem you would never publish, a poem for no audience.

But what if all this time, she asked no one, the audience has been keeping her alive?

Only an MD can prescribe. A poet can only describe.

Moment & moment, room & rooms ago, the MD asked the boy, Have you had thoughts of—and if you have, are the thoughts specific or abstract? She knew the right answer to that.

*Don't* be specific, she had never told a student.
Spare me the details, she had never told a student.

Maybe, she says to those assembled, writing is not about writing better. Maybe writing is about living better or maybe just living. Sometimes, she says, One cries out as Bob Creeley did "love, if you love me, lie next to me" and no one is there. Perhaps you're here to learn to write in/of/for those moments when no one is there. To learn the words to use/to mean/to be/to feel so alone.

We are living at a time, someone said.
We are living in a time, someone said.

When the MD asks for family history, she thinks, no son should hear his mother say [      ] but he needs to know. Also, the MD: which dosage, what kind, when, why.

She has written about this but about herself. Is there/who is her-*self*? When did she become *she* has never felt so unself—is she I? The boy is a minor for fourteen days more. His molecules hardly in her motherbiome anymore. After which he will be allowed to sit in rooms like these without her but will always be her child, will still be the almost-man he is, until he is a man.

She is moving away. She explains with words: this & that moment & moment: about the father who is at work, who at night no longer lies next to her which may be diagnostic. The other sons who may be diagnostic.

She cannot see everything or can she? She can see how utterly beautiful by which she means all the fucked-up, mistaken, broken lot of them.

"When the first baby arrived he was so little she began to have enemies," wrote Sarah Vap.

This boy—the boy, her boy—who came from the room of her body in which she & the man who made him with her had held the boy, rocked him, even when he didn't like it. Sometimes sleeping, sometimes screaming, the rooms & rooms of books & moments, two brothers, mother-&-fatherful rooms in which she'd watched him & made poems of/from/for/out of his words/his body of/from/for/out of her mothermindheart-biome.

Rooms, moments, in which she'd stopped making poems, stopped making dinner, making love, making herself into any-thing, to pry a button from his toothless mouth, lay him back down, pick him up, change him, sing songs in languages she didn't even know, pretend, pretend, pretend to—  Numbers, sippy cups, food, pen & paper, distraction, costumes, stories. At-tend, attend, pay & pay & *pay attention*, wait, watch. You seem ... are you? am I? We are going to sit here until you feel better/stop crying/go to sleep/get dressed/finish that home-work/tell me what's wrong/find another way to say that/tell your brother you're sorry, look at me when I speak to you.

Here is the bomb upon which to throw her unremitting vig-ilance, her body that is almost beyond childbearing years. But the bomb is everywhere. It is the rain, the despond, harvest, magnitude & bond. She cannot stop the bomb, the bond, the rain, this pain, down & down & down upon them.

Blood of my blood of my innermost blood, it is not my turn to answer: "Would you ever?"

The answer in every language at every moment must be: *never.*

Never, never, never, never. It has come to my attention that the world is a mortal/miraculous/terrible place & yours is not my life to make or take.

# THE MOON IS IN HER CAUL TONIGHT

Tomorrow I'll wake at dawn & try to see the partial lunar eclipse
but right now I can't stop watching Allen Ginsberg on youtube
not slapping William F. Fuckley upside his dumb white face in
1968 long enough to go check out the blood blue supermoon,
can't turn away from Ginsberg's balding beautiful bearded
countenance, can't stop loving his rage against police brutality
& the incarceration-persecution of Lenny Bruce who Ginsberg
tells Buckley was offering "Swiftian satire" & "political evi-
dence." Oh Allen, I say to no one, Here I am alone in the woods
in White America. This little shtetl—I mean shelter—I mean
studio—where some fifty years later our people have risen &
fallen into whiteness.

But when my personal hot spot falters—Ginsberg & Buckley
freeze in their places, Ginsberg's long hair from this angle like
a mess of payis. I turn on a podcast & there's Danez Smith
laughing & saying to Franny Choi, Girl, white people are listen-
ing! I *am* listening, I say to no one in the white woods in my
whiteness. Then the heat kicks on & I can't hear Danez.

I traipse outside—long down coat over pajamas—my little flashlight & flight of kush to see for myself & the moon looks like the moon. Perhaps a bit brighter or whiter than usual but no blood as far as I can see. I shiver back inside & find the hot spot back on, Ginsberg singing Hare Krishna, lovingly pumping his harmonium.

January 30, 2018 & Dia da Saudade is drawing to a close. The moon through the pane is blurred by something I can't define.

My mother is/was dead by now five years ago even though the report of death abroad marks January 31, 2013, as the day they turned off the machine that could no longer pump blood & oxygen to her heart & lungs.

That Doug wants a poem from me might be all that ties me to the earth this night, might be what keeps me breathing quietly seething: I uck you, you big-deal moon, where is your blood? where is your blue? where is your anything but white? You're too full of yourself tonight shining down on us & cold. Nothing will warm us if the history of insidious behavior turns out to be just human nature. In a few hours my father on the Upper West Side will wake up & pray facing a wall he can't see for who knows what but not, I bet, for his dead ex-wife. Meanwhile no

211

one in town knew where I could buy a yahrzeit candle so I have only this soi-disant supermoon to light my grief & say kaddish with me.

Sheindel Yehezkiel Ruth & Harry, can you hear me? Have you in death returned to Poland Antwerp & Newark New Jersey? If so who will help me here in New Hampshire hold my great goddess mother in the light? Beautiful huntress, she was always too much for me. I hurl my love into the air, calling upon the living in whom I only occasionally believe, to *listen*. And you, what would you have me do, Allen? You would have been less interested in me than in any young boy. Not just because my bleeding middle-aged womanhood waning fertility body. Truth is I spend too much time in bougie anthologies & wifi libraries & even the dead know there's a war on. It's the same & different war you fought & lost.

The snow falls & falls on the frozen ground. The sky dilates & effaces. Do you know how many placentas I mean poems I've made in my lifetime? Some were like flowers, a slowly gathering female harmonium of orgasmic expression. Some sustained no one & were but the abrupted, aborted, stillborn materials of conception that unbecame me. Tonight I try to conjure small clitoral bulbs buried deep below the rock-hard terra while

Allen Ginsberg sings Hare Hare Hare Krishna. How I love to hear Ginsberg singing & saying, I'm not so sure about the original sin thing you want to push on everyone.

Allen says, The great secret is no secret & reads "Wales Visitation."

O Mother, No harm on thy body! says Allen Ginsberg. Smelling the brown vagina-moist ground, harmless, tasting the violet thistle-hair, sweetness, declaims Allen Ginsberg.

And when Allen Ginsberg tells Buckley to stop protecting all the old aunts of America from "the clubs of language and the blood of words that's running out of people's heads" the camera lingers on Allen's well-worn boots as if to discredit him. Allen, I love your dusty shoes & blue socks but your jeans are too short & Peter Orlovsky should have snipped that stray thread before letting you go on television.

But, wait, what was that unearthly glimmer? Who goes there? Allen, are you with her in the afterlife or have you been reborn? Can you hear me in these white woods praying *saudade, Maman*? I'm losing what I never had & finding what I have is loss. Is it you of blessed memory or some avenging revenant?

Mother, I meant no harm, no harm on thy body. Is that you in the nimbus? If so take pity on your only child. I am afraid & alone, tied off by night from the sun's umbilical attention. I don't know it yet but at dawn when I wake & go out into the white world, the moon will slip below the tree line just before she partially eclipses & I will miss her. I will miss her.

# THERE ARE TWO MAGICS

he said, describing the fantasy novel he was reading as they
walked the drizzled streets. She was listening & laughing & re-
alized she'd been walking through one city or another next to
this man for more than twenty years, longer of course than
their kids were old, their smart-alecky sons who hadn't yet met
the person with whom they might walk through rain discussing
ridiculous books with great sincerity & pleasure.

Seriously, he said, I can't stop reading it. But when they went
upstairs to the good bed, in the good hotel, he *did* stop reading
& found the place where her shoulder met her neck & touched
it until her mind finally went away for a while & they became
bedraggled. He went out like a light. But not even the good bed
at the good hotel after good sex could put her to sleep. Not the
meditation app or the long online essay about the white su-
premacy of conceptual poetry. She missed her dead mother &
her middle-aged cousin who'd died the summer before. She
wondered whether, miles away, her youngest was whimpering,

her oldest awake texting, her middle son worrying. She wanted the Husband to tell her the plot again but didn't want to wake him. He lay over the covers on his back, his breath audible & regular, folded hands rising & falling, peaceful & fearless, as if she'd never once meant him harm, as if she'd always loved this warm animal, as if this were not the same summer she'd said, If that's really how you feel this isn't going to last. And he hadn't said anything.

Anger sadness doubt & disappointment was a wave that slapped them down & under. So many people had died & life felt shorter than how long they'd been together. They had, through so many omissions & commissions, hurt & been hurt. It was that same summer but she was alive & awake. He was asleep & alive. They were weak but they were still there.

## WE CANNOT MAKE THEM HAPPY BEHAVE PASSIONATE PATIENT SAFE SORRY

Here! we say, except when we
Just a minute, we say, Hold on, we cry
We are calling, calling for, out for
Anyway have no money time book mind patience, we have
    lost it
We menarched menarched menarched to the beat
Now we peri we pause we post we meno
Huddling in bathrooms, we are texting not resting
Reading, not reading, we are actually
Not huddled, we are hiding
We are along [sic], pretending to be alone
Take this, we say to each other
Try this, we say
Try to stop trying, we say
Just as a thought experiment
Rename the pills, we say

With this pill I withstand the onslaught of testosterone

With this pill i [sic] am able to withstand the sight of my childr's
[sic] suffering

With this rancid sublingual I will remember to

Try try try try try to

Say: That was a terrible summer when

It is still that season, still that terrible

We say, Whatever is happening say it in past tense, that makes
it easier

In AA they say ... we say

In labor we said ...

We can't remember what we said in labor, never wrote it down

We make syllabi for & syllabi for & syllabi for

We enter the crying room & stay

We say I cannot affoard [sic] to go to the crying room all the
time

i [sic] will pretend I am not always everlastingly in the crying
room

We say, Remember the years we spent in the crying room?
when we are still in the crying room

We are still, we are moving, we are still moving, but barely

We make mind-boxses [sic] & climb in & farther in

We say, Would you like to join me in giving up control for one
week, day, hour, moment

We say, Yeah I don't know what that means either

We pray or we do not pray

We dance whildy [sic] to the summer's pop offering until we see the video & sit here stunned

We tiny bit want to go to hsopital [sic] until we are in it

No part of us at all wants to be in any real hospital

It is too quiet, it is too loud, there is a buzzing, a humming, a clanging, a rattling

We cannot afford the steps to the bathroom in the creaky house at night

And when the alarm goes off at three a.m. it is not a chirping, it is *full on*

No one wakes up or everyone wakes up, we cannot reach the reset

Men arrive to push the button, leave a grimy mark on the wall, say, If it happens again ...

There is no ladder, there is a ladder, where was it

There is a humming, a hissing, a groaning, a typing

There is not enough, there is too much, it went moldy, never got ripe

It is too early, too late, we cannot afford the small light of the device

We cannot listen to anything louder than rain or watch anything lighter than pitch dark at night for fear of waking anyone

We know, we know, believe us, we know

Turns out you *can* talk to us like that

Turns out you do all the things we meant when we said, We do
not act like that

Them, who used to be *of us*

Them, who are everything so now we are nothing

We are husks

We are sorry to hear you feel like this, we say to one another

We say, It will not always be this way

We say, We are listening

We are diminishing

The news says

The small white pills are for

This stretch of suffering is

We say, Drink more water if you can

Keep typing here, we say, BRB, sorry, sorry

Sadness is a luxury you can no longer

The rage is a fog, it is not a fog, it is fire, it is not, it is the ocean,
it is not, it is nothing, it is *full on*

Might be humidity, particulate, an insect or malfunction, say
the men who test the machine at 4 a.m.

All seems safe, quiet now, lights flashing, no siren

Ma'am, the men call you

You were smart to call, the men say

No problem at all, they smudge the wall

You might need a new device, the men say

It is seasonal, the air quality, sometimes no one knows

We must all keep calling, we tell one another

Keep calling, writing, menarching the senators congress

We say, Can you believe

The pop song means

It means

We cannot affoard [sic] the middle of the night

We are the water heater is leaking we only discover by reporting
the intermittent rumbling

Thought that was normal, we say

No that's not normal, what is normal anyway

Get that checked out, we say

Just checking in, we say

Give it a day, a years [sic], can you give in to it if you can't
change it

How long does it take to know somthing [sic] is amiss when ev-
erything is

Our jaws cannot unclench

We feel pain in & in our, all the time, suddenly suspiciously pre-
dictably

We say, I know this sounds ridiculous but

Just pretend you are a male professor and say something in-
comprehensible

It works every time, we say to one another, Try it

Can you make the typing sound like rain

Can you make the water of the whole ocean

We cannot afford punctuation

We cannot afford the listserv

We cannot afford not to

We are here, we say but we are not

We are hiding for one minute, We only asked for one minute,
    We never asked for

We are in plain sight in the kitchens where no one sees us

We are not gods but with our mighty hands we

With our mighty outstretched overstretched hands, with our
    weak, with our weeks

We reach retch wretches almost each

We know we are breaking we know

*We know*

I've got you, we say, Got your back, By your side

We say holding the space but it is too much space no space

We say holding you in the light but have no light are all hands
    have no hands

We are so light we nothing

Hold on, we say

A holding pattern, we say

Hold up, we say, Hold everything

We are sweating, it is not hot

We are cold now in the extremities always in extremity

Call anytime, my cell is just, text me

We put white pellets under our tongues or gallons of infusions

We hold the plank, lie in bed but for just one minute, get up,
   *get up now*

We walk & walk & walk & walk

Rest, we say to one another, Be still, Let your thoughts

The therapist says ... we say to one another

Call anytime, anytime, who has any time

My male colleages [*sic*], we say

Speaking of which, we say

They are lucky to have you, we say

We say all the things we cannot say to the male colleges [*sic*]
   to one another

We are a lot like money, we say

If we were gone

It would be

There would be no

What would they

But we cannot remember how to finish our own sentences

We are mid-

It is still now, even if we pretend this is the past

Hold on, we say

Hold on, we will be right back

Hold on, we are with you, we say but are not

We are right here, we say even though that's hardly true

We are alone we are never alone we are always

We are always we are always we are always

We are mothers because we made them that's why

We are mothers & we are frailing [*sic*] furrowed hollowed &
    trenched out

# RESIDENCY

At breakfast a writer says, An avocado is a good idea.

This seems true. As true as anything, which is to say, not true at all. An avocado, after all, is not an idea. Or is it?

Are you settling in?
Are you working like crazy?
Don't you just love it here?

Are you writing? everyone asks.
Is this writing? she wonders.

Adjusting, she says, to anyone who will listen. She tries/is trying/tried not to complain but all language is complaint or praise or prayer as she once told her students & she's stuck in complaint. The food, the sleeplessness, the unreliable wifi . . .

It's *good* for your sons not to be able to reach you right now, says the writer who thinks an avocado is a good idea.

No, it is *not* good for them, I says, meanly, actually speaking those words aloud. But thank you for your fantasy of what my motherhood is like, I manages not to say.

I writes—only to herself, in her mind—"mothers hurt other mothers sometimes" & crosses it out & in the mental margins, mental-writes "be kind," crosses it out, mental-writes "why?!" crosses it out, mental-writes, "you don't know her and she does-n't know you." I crosses it out & crosses it out. The mental word space is a gray roiling static. The mental word space is a record of the first thing she has written, albeit mental, albeit crossed out, since she has been here, but today is day two & she is not supposed to be writing.

Jenny George told her not to. At the last residency, her first, Jenny George said someone told her not to work for the first 25% of any residency. Just rest.

I does not know what rest looks or sounds like—silence? Like mental static? Like writing crossed out over & over again? I is so sick of her own thoughts, so sick of only having mean things to say or write. Complain, praise, pray—God help her she does not believe in God but God knows she would like to engage in gratitude once in a while, that's a prayer, I guesses. Does that make it writing? Is I? Writing?

I cannot believe the food here, says an artist. This artist normally lives in a place I just visited & hated where one of her unhappy sons is now unhappily living. Now the artist lives *here*, does the artist? Where does an artist live? Where is "here"? When is "now"? These are words that only exist in writing—*stop writing*—but if I stops writing then anyone (who are you?) lives nowhere, at no time, outside narrative, nothing.

I *love* bacon, the artist says.
Are you getting a ton done?
Is this your first time?
Vermont cheese!

My pronoun, she thinks, is I.
Sometimes she, she thinks. Sometimes we. Sometimes they.
Never he.
No one asks her her pronouns here. There is no *here*.
No one asks.

When unhappy son calls, I's phone buzzes. She is not supposed to have it on in the dining hall but she always does because the wifi doesn't work where she sleeps & she's not allowed to take calls where she works.

Call you back in 5? I texts.

**Well I have therapy at 9 so no**
**But it's ok**

**I can step out and talk now if you want**

**Nope it ok [*sic*]**

Did you say you're from Brooklyn?
Are you fiction or poetry?
Don't you love it here?
Are you visual? No? Writing?
I'm from the Uncanny Valley, she says.
Yeah, all poets live in Brooklyn, an artist explains to another art-
ist.

Do I love it here? she wonders. She does not know what that
means.
Where is here? What is here? Who is you?

The wifi is waiting at the studio where she is supposed to be
writing or not writing. No rest for the weary—haha, *wicked*, she
thinks.

No rest for wicked poets, I says out loud. I is not supposed to speak aloud in the studio. "Voices carry," they told her, on the orientation tour. Stop writing in your head, I says & shushes her own thoughts.

Don't worry, I says to anyone, I is not writing. There is no time. Or, no time outside of writing. Also, no time for writing. I makes a calendar of evenly spaced empty boxes on a large sheet of thick beige paper using a ruler, sharp pencil, math & eraser, then sits down to read.

"Save it / for a shitty poem like a normal / wretch," writes Tommy Pico in *IRL*.

"Boundaries / aren't cages. Meter / is a fine flute. / But maybe nobody wants / to hear you. Maybe / you are just an asshole," writes Tommy Pico in *IRL*.

I walks to the nearby grocery store to buy more avocados, a jar of tahini & a bar of dairy-free chocolate.

For the fiftieth episode of her podcast (which she needs to sound edit) her least unhappy son introduces & briefly interviews her before Yanyi & then her husband interview her for a kind of "turning the mics" special. The boy is very young, very astute. He says in his high, almost genderless voice: You tend to be interested in things that are very abstract or things that are amazingly specific. It can kind of work for any form of art, like that painting over there . . . it doesn't have an image in it that's clear . . . but you also really like photography & that almost always has an image . . .

what if I came home this saturday, texts unhappy son who is unhappily living far from home

Great! I texts
want to talk on phone?

[no response]

I'm available on phone or text, I texts

[no response]
[no response]

is that perhaps too much availability for you? I texts

Son calls. I answers, rushing down the stairs, putting on boots & stepping out (I is not supposed to speak on phone in studio) into the cold rain & no wifi &—

**Lost you**, I texts.

**Call me back?** Son texts.

1 **minuets** [*sic*], I texts, moving toward what she thinks is wifi.

Son texts a jpeg of Minuet in G for piano & violin by J. S. Bach (1685–1750).

Two hours later she has heard all about the Ezra Klein podcast her son listens to which this morning was about rat studies. Her son says rats, given a choice between water & heroin-water, drank themselves to death with heroin-water except someone said well these are not normal rat conditions because the original study had rats isolated & when they redid the study allowing rats normal rat behavior including, importantly, sex with other rats & rat cavorting, the rats never got addicted to heroin-water & didn't suicide themselves to heroin death.

So, that's about rats, says her son, who is unhappily living in a city he hates where he doesn't know anyone. Also, he tells I, white upper-middle-class women in the 1950s were all on drugs & painkillers & wondering hey why do I feel like shit because they thought they were living the dream if the dream was a husband who doesn't beat you & all you had to do is stay home & keep house & raise children. Why do I feel so rotten? they asked the doctors who then prescribed them . . .

So that's about rats, her son says.
Also: solitary confinement, her son says.
Just come home, she says.
What should I tell my boss? he asks.

You know what to tell him, I says, but stands in the rain outside the studio for another forty-five minutes & they talk about this & about rats & about his plane ticket & they decide he will wait a few hours before talking to his boss & see how it feels to sit with the idea of coming home on Saturday.

"No sun / without shadow No night / without annihilation No morning / without assimilation No / Star to row towards / No myth to speak / for us. Just bodies," wrote Tommy Pico.

Ten minutes later her son texts:

**Boss says fine, OK.**

Don't worry, Jenny George, it is time for lunch. Who is she talking to? Jenny George is nowhere. Jenny George is not here. Not now. Not unless she writes her into here, into now but Jenny George said not to, remember? She texts Jenny George:

**thinking of you**

Then, perhaps because she is incapable of writing anything other than complaining, or because she is incapable of not writing, she texts Jenny George:

**Trying to have an open mind but so far HATE it here. Was going to try to have my first 2 days here rest days just like you said but I'm so stressed out I don't even know how to rest or what you even meant by that! All food has dairy. No reliable wifi not even getting texts super worried about my kids older two still struggling am making i suspect enemies or at least not friends. Can't remember why anyone ever liked me**

How restful it is, all this not-writing. Haha. Liar. Liar, liar, writer.

At lunch, which is sausage in cream sauce over buttered noodles, I asks the only male person at the table: What was it like to be the only male writer in the room at the optional writers-only get-together last night?

I'm used to it, he says.

She should have said, the night before, at the writers-only optional meeting, No feedback, please, when she'd volunteered to read first & a writer had asked, Do you want feedback?

I tries to explain all this to he & to the two artists at the table. It takes all of lunch to explain what she thinks about feedback & criticism & trust & workshop & literary theory & pedagogy & I knows she is coming across very badly & I is also rudely distracted because waiting for Delta "Good Goes Around" Air Lines to return her call about unhappy son's ticket.

I's phone buzzes as I is walking back to studio. It is the unhappy son who is living far from home but planning to go home Saturday for good & has just quit his job.

**I feel honestly worried that this is EXACTLY how**
**people decide to kill themselves**
**Is that reasonable**
**It's not, is it?**
**It builds up for a long time**
**And then people make the decision over the course of**
**a day or a day and a half**

WHAT?! I responds, stepping in a puddle, almost tripping on the sidewalk.

An hour's worth of texts later—is this writing—are you writing?—(Laurel calls I can't answer)—phew, I feels son is safe enough to stay where he is till Saturday.

Tommy Pico: "What kind of artless / simpleton says what they / truly feel? It's hard / to quote know unquote / what you want."

I texts Husband. I works on podcast. In podcast Yanyi says one thing he likes about I is that she likes to "sweep all the corners." I sound edits. The over-the-ear headphones make the stems of I's glasses dig into her head.

James is helping Sharon. Nicholas is at work. Christine has a call she has to take. No one can say how much editing, if any amount, will make this a workable episode. James at the chiropractor. Nicholas at work. Christine walking her dog.

FYI: I is doing all of this sober. That is to say, all of whatever "it" is that I is doing, she does it sober. In case you were wondering.

Tommy Pico: "W/ / a friend, you will forget / to pay attention."

I cannot stop paying attention. W/ or w/o. Is this writing? (Stop writing.) Is this resting? Is not paying attention the same as not paying any mind, the same as not minding?

I needs to get her act together. Jenny George might be right about a lot of things, but I is on two panels the week after this, whatever these two weeks are—purgatory, freedom?—& whether I writes anything or not, rests or not, she better be ready for "Poetry and Power with Kaveh Akbar." Do we want a moderator & what will we be discussing? Will it be recorded? Am I the moderator? Shall we each read poems? Kaveh: no response. Also, the symposium on Allen Ginsberg in which I is supposed to speak for ten minutes about Allen Ginsberg on the "Out of Place" panel at the St. Mark's Poetry Project at 8 p.m. Friday, which is very close to the time that I is usually watching TV & then going to sleep. Can I read her poem, instead, the only poem she wrote at the last residency, the poem about Ginsberg & being out of place? Can I just read that, she asks Jameson, the organizer, instead of "prepared remarks" & what is a poem if not prepared remarks? Jameson: no response.

I emails famous poet Anne Waldman who is also slated to offer "prepared remarks" about Allen Ginsberg at the "Out of Place" panel to ask if Waldman would be willing to—yes! Waldman writes back: I know who you are of course and your important work!

Who is I talking to? This is so embarrassing! Who is I name-dropping Anne Waldman to? Well, it's too late now & if you must know, Anne Waldman was born in 1945 & it was recently her birthday. Anne Waldman's birthday according to wikipedia, which is brought to you by wifi, is April 2, 1945. And why is I looking that up & what does it mean to I that Anne Waldman would like to sit with you—by whom I means I—for two hours in a room & record a podcast conversation, well it means a whole lot so take that, anyone!

**He's coming home Saturday**, she g-chats Laurel. **Too depressed. Too lonely.**

**Sorry, hun,** Laurel responds.

**How are you?** I thoughtfully asks Laurel. (I is not a monster if you can believe that.)

**Im good overbusy,** messages Laurel who, upon hearing I's complaints, reminds I that she (Laurel) herself recently left a residency early.

Look here, if she's writing about Laurel, she must be writing & she is not supposed to be writing. It has been a long time since she has *not* put Laurel in a poem. Laurel who is her friend but lives in Atlanta & is never *here*, never *now* except always in her poems. I thinks, What's my deal with Laurel? & wonders if the only point of writing anything, ever, is so I can read it to Laurel, because when she asks Laurel hey can I read you something? Laurel usually says "Yes" or "Sure, as soon as I finish teaching and get in the car" or "Sure, as long as you don't mind if we get interrupted by the plumber's arrival."

Maybe I should sign up for the reading tomorrow & read what I is not-writing & stop all the time bothering Laurel who is overbusy but makes time for I anyway. Almost everyone I knows that she would like to read anything to is a mother & overbusy & there is no point writing unless I can read this to anyone.

**give me a call when you get a chance**, Doug texts.

Fast enough? I whispers into the phone, in the studio, where I is not supposed to be talking.

What are you doing this Saturday night? And are you in a library or something? Doug asks.

Good questions, she says but just then Delta "We Love to Fly and It Shows" Air Lines calls. Got to go, I says.

Other son calls. Other son calls.

"Everything is so extra, / it gets hard / to know what to actually / give a fuck about," writes Tommy Pico.

I finishes *IRL*. Christine is ready to talk podcast but dinner is now or never & probably smothered in dairy.

> **BRB** she slacks @christine
> **OK but will prob be making dinner then** slacks back @christine

At dinner, which is manicotti & cream of tomato soup, two writers are so young, they are so young. They seem very smart but it may be a function of their youth & easy recall of words & ideas. They are friends or they are friendly or both. One of them is talking about babies & I says too much. I is editing in her head but everything is coming out despite the editing. No, a tiny, tiny fraction is coming out but it is still too many words, the kind of words not worth writing (I is not writing but I is writing in her head), maybe not even worth saying at the dinner table. I doesn't want to be that middle-aged poetmom going on & on about babies et al. as if that is her one field of expertise as if she knows all there is to know about babies but there she is.

Who told you you have to have a story? I had asked one of the young writers the night before at the optional writers-only get-together when this young writer read her very excellent pages from a novel-in-progress with first-person plural baby narrators & said she thought it should have "more of a story" so that people would "stay with her" but what she liked & had always liked was voice. The young, young writer says she spent the day changing everything to present tense & then back into past.

Maybe babies have a tense that is between past & present? I suggests & feels very smart, very wise, very old.

Baby tense! says the other young writer. They smile at I as if I is very quaint.

At the salad bar an artist is putting sriracha on his manicotti & Baba Yaga is using her fingers to take pieces of romaine off her plate & put them back into the communal serving bowl. I always take too much, Baba Yaga explains. I is not sure if Baba Yaga recognizes I as the person who, earlier that day, helped Baba Yaga navigate a treacherously icy crosswalk & listened to Baba Yaga explain that "only soulless, rich people live in New York City"—Baba Yaga is the expert on New York City because she drove a taxi there for years before moving to California "where the weather is warm but the people are all stupid."

Back at the table the baby writers are gone & two artists & a writer have sat down next to I's empty plate & store-bought avocado. An artist asks a writer how old her puppy is & if she misses him desperately. Yes, says the writer, who tells everyone that in order to crate train the puppy she's taken to sleeping on the floor next to the crate because this is the only way the puppy feels safe enough to stop crying. The artist says, My dog is with my parents right now and I was so worried and sad but my mom sent me a photo of him smiling and now I wonder if he misses me at all. Another artist says, I feel so guilty but I just couldn't take it . . . we might foster for a while you know to work our way back into it . . . it just feels so wrong, so wrong not to have a dog, but you know . . . to lose two in two years . . .

Everyone at the table, except for I, has stopped eating & is sitting silently, one of them starting to cry. I is trying not to make any noise with her cutlery, but it's not so easy to be silent while trying to spear garbanzo beans.

They're like *children*, says an artist, They're *just* like *children*. (I realizes the artist is saying that dogs are like children, not that artists are like children which I thinks artists are.) Everyone, except for I, nods. I considers making a joke about how her children are like dogs, *just like dogs*, but are they? Would a better joke be "my children treat me like a dog?" Maybe, but her children don't treat her the way these artists & writers treat their dogs & anyway they wouldn't get the joke.

I'm not good at small talk either, says a writer, leaning across the two empty seats between them & touching I on the shoulder.

Vermont cheese! says an artist, arriving at the table with a plate full of buttered bread & slabs of cheese.

So, I heard you've been to the grocery store, says an artist, pointing at I's avocado. Yes, I says, That's where I get all my best ideas.

When her least unhappy son calls to tell his mother how un-
happy he is, I hurries out of the dining hall so she can hear him
explain that he is very, very, *very* unhappy & not only because
his team lost their game in round-of-16 elimination & will not
be going to the state cup, not only because he cannot find his
Stars Premier jacket which if he lost it is NOT his fault & he
needs it & Dad offered the other Stars Premier jacket but that
is the other one & has white on the shoulders & is not the same
& you don't get it at all it is *mandatory* to wear it to practice &
Dad keeps saying well what do you want me to do but obviously
someone has to do *something*, do you even know what man-
datory means? And his mother who happens to be I, wants to
go to the after-dinner artist slideshow presentation, which is
not mandatory & yes I knows what mandatory means, but I is
losing wifi sorry, good luck, hope you find it, sorry.

This was made with ball pen, says an artist.
This was made from the ephemeral after the earthquake, says
    an artist.
The background influences my work so I rip it up, says an artist.
This is a detail, says an artist.
This is silk overlaps ink, says an artist.
I treat it as a body so you feel the textures.

The boat demanded to be painted large.

I was trying to paint anticipation and the entire Northeast Corridor.

I'm making place and purpose and the quantity of vastness, says an artist.

I am making everything the size of my hand. I am making a small glacier.

If it breaks, says an artist, I rub it with oil and tie it back together.

I am interested in how water behaves, says an artist.

This is David, formerly incarcerated. This is a mock-up. This is David again, says an artist.

This is a tableau of shadows.

This is in acrylic. This is in oil. This is on paper.

The words are meant to be, says an artist, Hard to read.

I use animals as metaphors. I use people too, says an artist.

This is a painting about death. It is very small. No one bought this, says an artist.

This is a system of systems.

I'm a time-based artist, says an artist.

I put a level on a level on a level on a level until it cannot be flat, says an artist.

This is about leisure, efficiency, and futility, says an artist.

These are very small. They are hard to see. I do the folding first, says an artist.

Is it any better? the Husband asks, after the artist slideshow. And what are you doing there? You'd tell me, right, if you were *doing something*? I mean, are you really not doing *anything*?

The Husband & I are on the phone in I's bedroom where there is no wifi but yes phone service.

The Husband means writing when he asks is I "doing anything." He means is I saying I'm not writing but meanwhile is writing a masterpiece or any-piece or even any piece of garbage & later will I say "oh I didn't do anything except for this [      ] . . ." And [      ] will turn out to be amazing & so therefore it's possible the Husband might be feeling bad for I for no reason right now.

Well, says I, I'm taking all the line breaks out of all my poems.
Why? says the Husband, sounding alarmed.
I'm tired of being reviled, I says. Even I hate poets, I says.
Huh, says the Husband, sounding skeptical.
You never read the poems on the page anyway, just hear them out loud, I says, So what do you care about the line breaks?
Yeah, but what are you doing *all day*? the Husband asks again.

I says to the Husband, (trying, as always, to be honest), Today I:

Went to meditation room for 7:30 meditation, no one there, not even me, sat cross-legged on bolster for seven minutes, couldn't manage ten, kept peeking at watch, struck a metal bowl—

Went to breakfast, unpleasant interaction, avocados are either fruits or vegetables but not ideas—

Helped an old woman navigate icy path & listened to her spew vitriol, probably my karma for earlier being not nice to different older woman—

Bought $3 almond-milk cortado & considered but came to no conclusions about the origin of coffee man's extreme hostility—

Tommy Pico—

Text with son—

Two-hour conversation with son who is coming home Saturday btw—

Text with son—

Texted you (in this case Husband)—

Delta "On Top of the World" Air Lines automated services (one hour)—

Tommy Pico—

Lunch where I asked only male writer here how did it feel to be the only male writer at the writers-only group last night—

Finished Tommy Pico—

Emailed Tommy Pico want to be on podcast?—

Delta "Keep Climbing" Air Lines canceled old ticket for son & returned miles no charge medical emergency but deposited miles into wrong account—

Texted son—

Texted Husband ("you")—

Texted sons—

Not enough miles to buy new ticket—

Texted Husband—

Emailed Patricia Smith—

Emailed Kaveh Akbar—

Emailed Anne Waldman—

Artist slideshow presentation . . .

The Husband is not paying attention. Instead wants to tell her about the Jewish meeting at school which was very upsetting & other son's misbehavior & other son's lost jacket & fine he will buy the ticket with more miles & everything is fine says the Husband & if it's not fine what can we do anyway? Do I want to just come home? And am I *really* not writing? Or am I secretly writing? Also, does anyone there even know who I am?

I is not really paying attention because I has started taking photographs of the bedroom: the hook on the wall above the bed, the lamp, the corner of the room, the light coming in under the door, the doorstop, the fire alarm, the outlets, the lightbulbs, her reflection in the dark window. I wishes she had a real camera, not just her phone because I has the feeling now—she is not listening, she is *seeing*. She is seeing something very abstract, something very specific. She is sweeping all the corners, even if she doesn't quite know what that means. The Husband has said goodnight & hung up, but I barely noticed/notices. This is the kind of time that is present & past (maybe Baby Time or what Stein called the continuous present)—it is not writing exactly but it is also not resting . . . oh my, I is caught red-handed when—

Jenny George texts! This is a small miracle because texts have not been coming through. It is almost enough (not really) to make I believe in God.

> **It's good that you're getting another chunk of time away with your work! Sometimes in a situation like this I just decide I'm not going to make friends, then if I don't, I've met my goal. And if I do, I'm pleasantly surprised**, texts Jenny George.

> **I love this text. Thank you**, I texts

I pulls three tarot cards from the deck, having forgotten to do so first thing that morning. Where I is coming from: Seven of Swords. Where I is: Eight of Cups. Where I is going: Queen of Cups.

**How was it for you tonight?** Jenny George texts.

I texts back: **Well the day was pretty bad and then I went to an artist slideshow and sat in the back writing down things artists said—I love how visual artists speak. I got an idea I want to make a poem/slide-show/movie/audio piece of my day and of the things people said to me and the texts I got and the book I read and the things I overheard and the things I saw sort of very Bernadette Mayer but also not and for the past hour I've been taking photos of my room . . . so . . . Ok? Or not? Or something?**

I photographs the tarot cards instead of looking at them carefully. She will figure out tomorrow, when she has more energy, more time, what they mean. Will I ever *have* time? TIme isn't a thing anyone has except that, if I writes, it has to be in a time— present tense, past tense, future tense, baby tense—& this is the only way to have/mark/make time, even if that is also the only way I spends/wastes/uses it.

**Sounds like a very solid day two! For me, anxiety and loneliness is the \*sign\* that I'm in proximity to my work**, texts Jenny George.

I watches the end of an episode of *The Affair*. Or, rather, I still-shots the movie as it plays on her laptop while she listens through headphones. I is not having An Affair, only watching a TV show about one & really she is not even really watching it, she is watching herself watching it, or watching herself not writing (which is to say writing). She is not sure whether this qualifies as "doing something" & therefore whether she inadvertently lied to the Husband.

From down the hall she can hear that woman with her dry cough—cough cough cough—as if she were in the room with her. And if she can hear anyone—artist, writer, who even knows—enter the building, clomp up the stairs, open & close the bathroom door, then anyone must have heard every word of her conversation with the Husband (including her litany of complaints & personal aspersions). Voices carry after all, hence the headphones.

I hasn't told the Husband about *The Affair* but he'll know soon enough when the itunes bill comes through that she bought seasons one, two & three. I starts the next episode only to discover, you've *got* to be kidding, that the show, which she thought was about *sex* (marital & extra-), turns out to be about the husband's "novel" about his affair & about how his lover & ex-wife feel about being represented in what "Noah" swears is fiction, not to mention the thinly veiled "Lockhart brothers" who want to beat the crap out of "Noah" for exposing their drug-ring ranch business out in Montauk. Wherever you go, there you are, she thinks & snaps her laptop shut.

I wonders if she should show the photographs she is taking along with an audio recording that she has not yet made or the genre-nonconforming prosem she has not yet written/is not-writing right now at the reading tomorrow. She is not supposed to write anything, she is supposed to be resting. And does anyone really want to know the answer to Do you love it here? If she shows the photographs she's taking will she allow herself to use filters? Yes, I thinks, she will! She will allow herself to do whatever the fuck she wants to these photographs of tarot cards, the snakelike lightbulbs, the creepy hook over the bed, the outlets that look like screaming robot faces, her reflection in the mirror, window, computer screen & finally, when she closes the laptop, the light pouring under the door into the not dark enough room. I will do anything she wants because writing is about truth (#NoFilters) but I is not writing.

I can't not-write in the dark so she makes notes on the phone. What if you could record everything? Charles Bernstein asked Bernadette Mayer in an interview they recorded years ago, which is always now when you listen to it. And Bernadette said—somewhat surprising Bernstein, I thinks—I would!

Bernadette? You should know who Bernadette is. You? Yeah, *you*. There is no writing without writing *to*. Therefore *you*. Audience, I'm sorry to drag you into this but you're always awake, that's the best thing about you. Bernadette Mayer is probably asleep. Charles Bernstein too. I hope Laurel is. And Jenny George.

I can't make notes on the phone without her glasses which have now fallen between the bed & the dresser which means there's a *here* which is between the bed & the dresser & a *now* which is the moment she is writing & not writing this poem which is not a poem. There's a *now* to write into, a continuous present that the act of writing stretches across a canvas so to speak & *into* or *onto* or *out of* this she presses record on the voice-recorder app & whispers into the phone:

> *Who are you talking to?*
> *The human voice carries.*

Anyway, it's after midnight. Anyway, is speaking writing?

"Meter / is a fine flute. / But maybe nobody wants / to hear you," wrote/written/write-ed Tommy Pico in real life in his book *IRL*.

She listens (recorder still on) & tries to record the sound of the woman's dry cough, of the noisy bed springs, of the downstairs front door opening & shutting.

Remember how in high school I often fell asleep while talking on the phone to my boyfriend or gossiping with Joan? Now, here, everything is a mirror—monitor, page, mic—recording the here & now. Expanded & collapsed entirely. Blink.

*Keep it down now, voices carry*, I whisper-sings in the dark, into the phone.
*Hush, hush, keep it down now. Voices carry.*

Do they? I wonders & repeats the refrain—*voices carry*—in self-admonition or is it wishful thinking?

Hush, she says.

*Light pours under the door*, I whispers, looking at the door.

If you can hear them, they can hear you.

A C K N O W L E D G M E N T S

Each book I write seems to require more, rather than less, help. For this book I received so much.

Thank you to the editors of the following publications that included versions of the pieces in this book: *The Nation*, *At Length*, The Academy of American Poets Poem-A-Day Series, *The Funk & Wag from A to Z* by Mel Chin, *Foundry*, *The Literary Review* & *American Poetry Review*.

Thank you to the Sustainable Arts Foundation, MacDowell Colony & Vermont Studio Center for support during the writing & editing of this book.

For reading, listening to, helping with & believing in this book (& in me): Craig Morgan Teicher, Laurel Snyder, Erika Meitner, Arielle Greenberg, Claudia Rankine, D A Powell, Joy Katz, Katy Lederer, Jennifer Kronovet, Christine Larusso, Nicholas Fuenzalida, Isaac Miller & everyone at Wave Books, especially Heidi Broadhead—thank you for your attention, patience, understanding & brilliance.

For your humor, advice, mothering & many hours of listening to me cry or crying with me: Erin Murray Marra, Joan Platt, Deirdre Lord, Monica Molenaar, Sharon Olds and the poetmoms listserv (founded & main-

**255**

tained by Arielle Greenberg). Thank you to my father, Benjamin Zucker, for his unfailing encouragement & enthusiasm. Thank you Jeremy Mindich and Daniel Shiffman for patient advice & for sticking with me.

Inarticulable, incalculable gratitude for Matthew Cruger, my therapist of many years & Peeka Trenkle, wisewoman, guide, mentor, spirit-counselor.

Thank you to each & every person named, mentioned or quoted in the book. I hope I have neither taken your names in vain nor made graven images.

Thank you to my students at New York University: your questions, opinions, poems, book recommendations & attention have made me a better teacher, writer, listener, thinker & human being.

Thank you to every guest of Commonplace—I learn so much from reading & speaking with you—& to the amazing Commonplace team: Christine Larusso, Nicholas Fuenzalida, James Ciano, Becca DeGregorio & Doreen Wang.

Some of these pieces are in memory of Diane Wolkstein, Daniel Mindich, Ilana Stein, Lotty & Charlie Zucker.

This book would be impossible without my husband of over twenty-two years, Joshua Goren. Moses, Abram & Judah: without you, I wouldn't know my real name; I love all of each of you *forever* & with all my heart.